Microsoft 365 Fundamentals Exam Prep

500 Practice Questions

Exam Code: MS-900

1st Edition

www.versatileread.com

Copyright © 2024 VERSAtile Reads. All rights reserved.
This material is protected by copyright, any infringement will be dealt with legal and punitive action.

Document Control

Proposal Name	:	Microsoft 365 Fundamentals Exam Prep: 500 Practice Questions
Document Edition	:	1st
Document Release Date	:	22 June 2024
Reference	:	MS-900
VR Product Code	:	20242102MS900

Copyright © 2024 VERSAtile Reads.

Registered in England and Wales

www.versatileread.com

All rights reserved. No part of this book may be reproduced or transmitted in any form or by any means, electronic or mechanical, including photocopying, recording, or by any information storage and retrieval system, without the written permission from VERSAtile Reads, except for the inclusion of brief quotations in a review.

Feedback:

If you have any comments regarding the quality of this book or otherwise alter it to better suit your needs, you can contact us through email at info@versatileread.com

Please make sure to include the book's title and ISBN in your message.

About the Contributors:

Nouman Ahmed Khan

AWS/Azure/GCP-Architect, CCDE, CCIEx5 (R&S, SP, Security, DC, Wireless), CISSP, CISA, CISM, CRISC, ISO27K-LA is a Solution Architect working with a global telecommunication provider. He works with enterprises, mega-projects, and service providers to help them select the best-fit technology solutions. He also works as a consultant to understand customer business processes and helps select an appropriate technology strategy to support business goals. He has more than eighteen years of experience working with global clients. One of his notable experiences was his tenure with a large managed security services provider, where he was responsible for managing the complete MSSP product portfolio. With his extensive knowledge and expertise in various areas of technology, including cloud computing, network infrastructure, security, and risk management, Nouman has become a trusted advisor for his clients.

Abubakar Saeed

Abubakar Saeed is a trailblazer in the realm of technology and innovation. With a rich professional journey spanning over twenty-nine years, Abubakar has seamlessly blended his expertise in engineering with his passion for transformative leadership. Starting humbly at the grassroots level, he has significantly contributed to pioneering the Internet in Pakistan and beyond. Abubakar's multifaceted experience encompasses managing, consulting, designing, and implementing projects, showcasing his versatility as a leader.

His exceptional skills shine in leading businesses, where he champions innovation and transformation. Abubakar stands as a testament to the power of visionary leadership, heading operations, solutions design, and integration. His emphasis on adhering to project timelines and exceeding customer expectations has set him apart as a great leader. With an unwavering commitment to adopting technology for operational simplicity and enhanced efficiency, Abubakar Saeed continues to inspire and drive change in the industry.

Dr. Fahad Abdali

Dr. Fahad Abdali is an esteemed leader with an outstanding twenty-year track record in managing diverse businesses. With a stellar educational background, including a bachelor's degree from the prestigious NED University of Engineers & Technology and a Ph.D. from the University of Karachi, Dr. Abdali epitomizes academic excellence and continuous professional growth.

Dr. Abdali's leadership journey is marked by his unwavering commitment to innovation and his astute understanding of industry dynamics. His ability to navigate intricate challenges has driven growth and nurtured organizational triumph. Driven by a passion for excellence, he stands as a beacon of inspiration within the business realm. With his remarkable leadership skills, Dr. Fahad Abdali continues to steer businesses toward unprecedented success, making him a true embodiment of a great leader.

Muniza Kamran

Muniza Kamran is a technical content developer in a professional field. She crafts clear and informative content that simplifies complex technical concepts for diverse audiences, with a passion for technology. Her expertise lies in Microsoft, cybersecurity, cloud security and emerging technologies, making her a valuable asset in the tech industry. Her dedication to quality and accuracy ensures that her writing empowers readers with valuable insights and knowledge. She has done certification in SQL database, database design, cloud solution architecture, and NDG Linux unhatched from CISCO.

Table of Contents

About MS-900 Certification 6
    Introduction 6
    What is MS-900? 6
    Benefits of MS-900 7
    Prerequisites for the MS-900 Exam 7
    The Intended Audience for the MS-900 Certification Course? 8
    The Certification Exam 8
    Exam Preparation 9
        Before Exam 9
        Day of Exam 9
        After Exam 10
    Exam Information 10
    MS-900 Exam Preparation Pointers 11
    Job Opportunities with MS-900 Certifications 12
        IT Support Roles 12
        User Administration and Management 12
        Sales and Business Development 12
    Demand for MS-900 Certification in 2024 13
Practice Questions 14
Answers 127
About Our Products 229

Copyright © 2024 VERSAtile Reads. All rights reserved.
This material is protected by copyright, any infringement will be dealt with legal and punitive action.

About MS-900 Certification

Introduction

This section introduces the MS-900 Microsoft 365 Fundamentals certification serves as a foundational credential for individuals aiming to establish their expertise in cloud services and productivity solutions within the Microsoft 365 ecosystem. This certification validates essential knowledge of Microsoft 365 services, including core concepts, security, compliance, and pricing. With its emphasis on cloud fundamentals, the MS-900 opens doors to various entry-level roles in IT support, user administration, sales, and business development. Additionally, it acts as a stepping stone to more advanced Microsoft 365 certifications, making it a valuable asset for those pursuing career growth in cloud-based technologies.

What is MS-900?

The MS-900 is the Microsoft 365 Fundamentals certification exam. It validates a candidate's foundational knowledge of cloud services and how those services are provided with Microsoft 365. The exam covers basic concepts of cloud computing, core Microsoft 365 services and concepts, security, compliance, privacy, and Microsoft 365 pricing and support. Passing the MS-900 exam demonstrates an understanding of cloud concepts and foundational Microsoft 365 services, making it a valuable credential for individuals beginning their journey in cloud services or seeking to validate their Microsoft 365 knowledge.

Benefits of MS-900

The MS-900 Microsoft 365 Fundamentals certification offers numerous advantages to individuals entering the realm of cloud services and productivity solutions. Firstly, it establishes a strong foundational knowledge of cloud computing concepts and core Microsoft 365 services. This serves as a solid groundwork for further specialization within the Microsoft 365 ecosystem. Secondly, MS-900 certification enhances career prospects by bolstering credibility with potential employers, potentially unlocking new opportunities in Microsoft 365-related roles. Thirdly, achieving MS-900 demonstrates a commitment to continuous learning and professional growth, garnering recognition from peers and industry stakeholders. Additionally, passing the exam validates proficiency in Microsoft 365 services, instilling confidence in one's ability to work effectively in cloud environments.

Moreover, MS-900 serves as a stepping stone to more advanced Microsoft 365 certifications, paving the way for career advancement. Furthermore, preparing for MS-900 fosters problem-solving skills and critical thinking, which are invaluable assets in cloud computing and productivity roles. Lastly, in a competitive job market, MS-900 certification sets candidates apart, providing a competitive edge and increasing their likelihood of securing interviews and job opportunities in the dynamic field of cloud services and productivity solutions.

Prerequisites for the MS-900 Exam

Prerequisites for excelling in the MS-900 exam don't demand an extensive background. However, a strong grasp of foundational cloud service concepts, particularly those related to Microsoft 365, is crucial. Familiarizing yourself with Microsoft 365 basics will significantly enhance your chances of success.

The Intended Audience for the MS-900 Certification Course?

The intended audience for the MS-900 Certification Course includes IT professionals new to Microsoft 365, aiming to acquire practical knowledge about Microsoft 365 services and their direct applications. Notably, scripting knowledge isn't a prerequisite; the focus is on using the Microsoft 365 admin center and related interfaces for managing services and resources. Additionally, students or beginners exploring Microsoft 365 job opportunities can gain the confidence needed to pursue further role-based Microsoft 365 programs, such as becoming a Microsoft 365 Administrator.

The Certification Exam

The MS-900 (Microsoft 365 Fundamentals) certification exam evaluates candidates' understanding and proficiency in fundamental concepts of cloud services with Microsoft 365. This comprehensive assessment aims to measure candidates' grasp of key principles, terminology, and practices related to Microsoft 365 cloud services.

- **Cloud Concepts and Principles:** This domain assesses candidates' comprehension of cloud computing concepts, including the benefits of cloud services, deployment models, and service models offered by Microsoft 365.
- **Core Microsoft 365 Services and Concepts:** Candidates are evaluated on their knowledge of essential Microsoft 365 services, such as productivity tools (e.g., Microsoft Office applications), collaboration tools (e.g., Teams, SharePoint), and their functionalities within the Microsoft 365 ecosystem.
- **Microsoft 365 Pricing and Support:** This domain focuses on candidates' understanding of Microsoft 365 pricing models, subscription options, and support plans available to Microsoft 365 customers.
- **Microsoft 365 Security, Privacy, Compliance, and Trust:** Candidates must demonstrate their knowledge of Microsoft 365 security principles, privacy controls, compliance standards, and trust

About MS-900 Certification

mechanisms implemented by Microsoft to safeguard Microsoft 365 services and data.
- **Microsoft 365 Governance and Compliance:** This domain assesses candidates' comprehension of Microsoft 365 governance methodologies, resource management techniques, and compliance considerations for managing Microsoft 365 resources effectively.
- **Microsoft 365 Service Level Agreements (SLAs) and Lifecycles:** Candidates are evaluated on their understanding of Microsoft 365 SLAs, service lifecycles, and maintenance practices to ensure the high availability and reliability of Microsoft 365 services.

Exam Preparation

Before Exam

To prepare for the MS-900 exam, it's essential to start by thoroughly reviewing the exam content outline provided by Microsoft. This outline delineates the domains and topics that will be covered in the exam, giving you a clear roadmap of what to focus on. Once you've familiarized yourself with the content, it's time to dive into study materials. Utilize a variety of resources such as textbooks, official Microsoft documentation, online courses, and practice exams to reinforce your understanding of Microsoft 365 fundamentals.

Day of Exam

On exam day, it's crucial to arrive early at the exam center to allow for check-in procedures and to settle in before the exam begins. Be sure to bring along all required documents, including valid identification and any other materials specified by the exam center. Once the exam starts, maintain a calm and focused mindset. Take deep breaths to help manage any nerves, and read each question carefully to fully understand what is being asked. Avoid feeling overwhelmed by difficult questions by staying focused and maintaining confidence in your abilities.

Managing your time effectively is essential during the exam. Pace yourself to ensure you have enough time to answer all questions thoroughly. If you

About MS-900 Certification

encounter particularly challenging questions, consider flagging them for review and returning to them later if time permits. By following these tips, you'll be better equipped to navigate the exam confidently and achieve success.

After Exam

After completing the exam, it's important to take time to reflect on your performance. Identify areas where you excelled and areas where there's room for improvement. If you have access to your exam results, review any questions you missed to understand why you answered incorrectly and learn from your mistakes. This reflection process helps solidify your understanding of the material and prepares you for future exams or real-world scenarios.

Exam Information

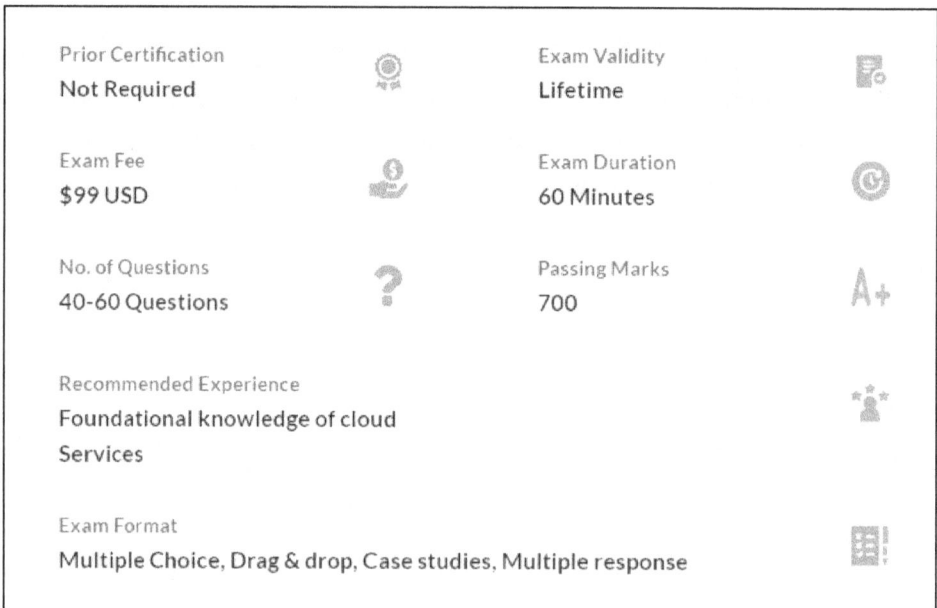

Prior Certification Not Required	**Exam Validity** Lifetime
Exam Fee $99 USD	**Exam Duration** 60 Minutes
No. of Questions 40-60 Questions	**Passing Marks** 700
Recommended Experience Foundational knowledge of cloud Services	
Exam Format Multiple Choice, Drag & drop, Case studies, Multiple response	

Copyright © 2024 VERSAtile Reads. All rights reserved.
This material is protected by copyright, any infringement will be dealt with legal and punitive action.

MS-900 Exam Preparation Pointers

Preparing for the MS-900 certification exam requires a structured approach to ensure readiness and confidence on exam day. Here are some tips to guide your MS-900 exam preparation:

1. **Understand the Exam Content:** Familiarize yourself with the domains and topics outlined in the MS-900 exam content provided by Microsoft. This will give you a clear understanding of what to expect on the exam and which areas to focus your study efforts on.
2. **Utilize Study Materials:** Make use of a variety of MS-900 study materials, including textbooks, official Microsoft documentation, online courses, and practice exams. These resources will help reinforce your understanding of Microsoft 365 fundamentals and provide insights into exam format and question types.
3. **Take Practice Exams:** Completing MS-900 practice exams is essential for assessing your knowledge and identifying areas that require further study. Practice exams simulate the exam environment and help you gauge your readiness while familiarizing yourself with the types of questions you may encounter.
4. **Create a Study Schedule:** Develop a study schedule that allocates time for reviewing each domain covered in the MS-900 exam content. Set realistic study goals and deadlines to keep yourself accountable and ensure thorough coverage of all exam topics.
5. **Join Study Groups:** Consider joining MS-900 study groups or online forums where you can engage with other exam candidates, share resources, and discuss challenging topics. Collaborating with peers can provide additional insights and support throughout your exam preparation journey.
6. **Stay Updated:** Keep abreast of developments in Microsoft 365 fundamentals by staying updated with industry trends, best practices, and emerging technologies. Attend relevant training sessions, workshops, and conferences to expand your knowledge and skills in this evolving field.
7. **Practice Time Management:** During the exam, manage your time effectively by pacing yourself and allocating sufficient time to answer

each question. Flag difficult questions for review and prioritize your efforts based on question weight and difficulty.

Job Opportunities with MS-900 Certifications

The MS-900 Microsoft 365 Fundamentals certification, while foundational, can open doors to various entry-level and foundational roles within the Microsoft 365 ecosystem. Here's a breakdown of some potential career paths:

IT Support Roles

- **Help Desk Analyst:** Providing initial technical support for users encountering issues with Microsoft 365 applications (e.g., email, documents, collaboration tools).
- **Microsoft 365 Support Specialist:** Assisting users with more advanced troubleshooting and configuration within the Microsoft 365 suite.
- **Desktop Support Technician:** Offering general IT support with a focus on troubleshooting Microsoft 365 applications alongside other desktop functionalities.

User Administration and Management

- **Microsoft 365 User Administrator:** Managing user accounts, permissions, and access within the Microsoft 365 environment.
- **Office 365 Administrator:** Provisioning and managing user accounts, licenses, and security settings for core Office applications within Microsoft 365.
- **Microsoft 365 Adoption Specialist:** Promoting user adoption of Microsoft 365 applications and functionalities within an organization.

Sales and Business Development

- **Microsoft 365 Sales Associate:** Leveraging your understanding of Microsoft 365 fundamentals to explain the benefits and functionalities to potential customers.

About MS-900 Certification

- **Cloud Solutions Specialist:** Understanding Microsoft 365 as part of a broader cloud solution offering, potentially including Azure services.
- **Business Analyst:** Utilizing knowledge of Microsoft 365 to analyze business needs and identify solutions that can be implemented within the platform.

Demand for MS-900 Certification in 2024

The demand for the MS-900 Microsoft 365 Fundamentals certification is expected to remain strong in 2024 for several reasons:

- **Widespread Microsoft 365 Adoption:** Microsoft 365 is a dominant force in the productivity suite market, with businesses of all sizes increasingly relying on its cloud-based applications. This widespread adoption fuels the demand for professionals with a foundational understanding of the platform.
- **Entry Point to Microsoft 365 Expertise:** The MS-900 serves as the launching pad for Microsoft 365 certification paths. Earning it demonstrates a basic grasp of the platform's functionalities and value proposition, making it valuable for anyone interested in pursuing a career focused on Microsoft 365 administration, support, or sales.
- **Validation of Basic Cloud Skills:** Even in non-technical roles, having the MS-900 showcases a basic understanding of cloud-based productivity tools, potentially giving you an edge in today's job market where cloud adoption is pervasive.

Practice Questions

1. At which point in the Office 365 registration process do you select your tenant name?
A. After you have selected your licenses
B. Immediately after supplying your name, phone number, and email address
C. After setting up your Exchange environment
D. Once all user accounts have been created

2. What is the default domain suffix for all Office 365 and Microsoft Azure tenants?
A. .office.com
B. .microsoft.com
C. .onmicrosoft.com
D. .azure.com

3. What happens if you select a tenant name that is already in use?
A. The process continues with a warning.
B. The system automatically assigns a different name.
C. You won't be able to proceed until a unique name is chosen.
D. You are charged an additional fee for a premium name.

4. Is it possible to change your tenant name after creating your Office 365 subscription?
A. Yes, at any time.
B. Only within the first 30 days.
C. No, it cannot be changed.
D. Yes, with a special request to Microsoft support.

Practice Questions

5. Where does the tenant name appear in Exchange Online?
A. Only in the email header for external messages.
B. In the routing email address for mail-enabled objects.
C. Only in the Exchange Online global address list (GAL).
D. It doesn't appear in Exchange Online at all.

6. How is the tenant name used in SharePoint Online?
A. It appears in the email header of messages sent from SharePoint.
B. It is used as the default administrator username.
C. It is visible in site content URLs and sharing URLs.
D. It is only used internally and not shown in URLs.

7. What is the significance of the @tenantName.mail.onmicrosoft.com address in Exchange Online?
A. It's the primary email address for users.
B. It's an optional service routing address.
C. It's the only email address that can send emails externally.
D. It's automatically added to every new user account.

8. What should be considered before creating your Office 365 tenant name in the context of company changes?
A. The possibility of changing it later.
B. The tenant name's relevance after merger, acquisition, or divestiture.
C. The number of user licenses you will need.
D. The type of subscription plans available.

9. Where does the tenant name appear in relation to OneDrive for Business?
A. On the login screen only.
B. In the OneDrive system files.

Practice Questions

C. In the sharing URLs and browser address bar.
D. It is not used in OneDrive for Business.

10. What is the email address ending in @tenantName.onmicrosoft.com used for in Exchange Online?
A. As the main contact email for Microsoft support.
B. As a mandatory routing address that cannot be changed.
C. For external communications only.
D. As an alias for user accounts.

11. Where can the tenant name in Skype for Business be found when reviewing meeting requests?
A. Within the email body text
B. In the email subject line
C. Inside the meeting agenda
D. In the meeting URL

12. Is the tenant name visible in the properties of Office Pro Plus applications?
A. Yes, it's always visible
B. No, it's not visible
C. Only in Microsoft Visio
D. Only in Microsoft Project

13. How does Office Online indicate the tenant's name when creating new documents?
A. Through a pop-up notification
B. In the document properties
C. In the browser address bar
D. It doesn't indicate the tenant's name

Practice Questions

14. What happens to an Office 365 trial subscription after 30 days if not upgraded?
A. It automatically renews
B. It switches to a Home Use plan
C. You must start paying or select another plan
D. The subscription gets extended for another 30 days

15. In the context of Office 365, what can be done during the trial subscription period?
A. Only account setup is allowed
B. Syncing users and assigning licenses is not permitted
C. Syncing users and assigning licenses to begin testing the service
D. Unlimited use of all features without restrictions

16. What are the four basic technologies present in Office 365?
A. Word, Excel, PowerPoint, OneNote
B. Exchange, Skype, SharePoint, OneDrive
C. Exchange, Skype, SharePoint, Office Pro Plus
D. Outlook, Teams, Access, Publisher

17. Which categories are Office 365 plans divided into?
A. Small Business, Education, Government, Nonprofit, Home Use
B. Professional, Enterprise, Student, Individual, Group
C. Basic, Standard, Premium, Ultimate
D. Core, Modular, Flexible, Custom

18. Why can't a single answer be given regarding the best possible Office 365 plan?
A. Plans are the same for all users
B. Office 365 only offers one type of plan

Practice Questions

C. Plans are constantly evolving and very complex
D. All plans are considered the best

19. What is the default save location for newly created documents in Office Online applications?
A. The device's local storage
B. SharePoint
C. OneDrive for Business
D. External storage devices

20. After the trial subscription expires, what options are available regarding the licenses?
A. The licenses get deleted
B. You can only renew the existing licenses
C. Renew the existing licenses or add different ones
D. Licenses automatically upgrade to premium

21. What is the maximum number of users you can have with Office 365 Business plans before considering an upgrade to Office 365 Enterprise?
A. 100 users
B. 200 users
C. 300 users
D. 400 users

22. Which feature is not included in Office 365 Business plans but is available in Office 365 Enterprise plans?
A. SharePoint Online Plan 1
B. 50 GB mailbox storage limit
C. Unified communications options like PSTN conferencing
D. Excel application

Copyright © 2024 VERSAtile Reads. All rights reserved.
This material is protected by copyright, any infringement will be dealt with legal and punitive action.

Practice Questions

23. What is the size limit for a shared mailbox in Office 365 before requiring an additional license?
A. 25 GB
B. 50 GB
C. 100 GB
D. Unlimited

24. Which Office 365 Enterprise plan includes Office Pro Plus, Exchange Rights Management, and eDiscovery Center?
A. Enterprise E1
B. Enterprise E3
C. Enterprise E5
D. Enterprise F1

25. What additional features does Office 365 Enterprise E5 include over the E3 plan?
A. 50 GB mailbox limit
B. Advanced eDiscovery and Customer Lockbox
C. 2 GB OneDrive for Business storage
D. Office Online applications

26. Which Office 365 Enterprise plan is targeted at users who do not need a full-featured workstation?
A. Enterprise E1
B. Enterprise E3
C. Enterprise E5
D. Enterprise F1

Practice Questions

27. For which type of organizations are Office 365 Nonprofit plans available?
A. Any small to medium-sized business
B. Government agencies
C. Nonprofit organizations
D. Educational institutions

28. Which Office 365 plan is typically free for students and teachers?
A. Office 365 Nonprofit
B. Office 365 Government
C. Office 365 Business
D. Office 365 Education

29. What might cause users to receive non-delivery errors when replying to old emails after migrating to Office 365?
A. Incorrect email address
B. Missing x500 address in the recipient's proxy addresses
C. Firewall blocking the emails
D. Outlook version incompatibility

30. Which additional compliance features are included in Office 365 Government plans?
A. Content is stored in the United States only
B. 1 TB OneDrive for Business storage
C. SharePoint Online Plan 1
D. Free access for students and teachers

31. Where in the Office 365 Admin Center can you view your current subscriptions?
A. Dashboard
B. Users

Practice Questions

C. Billing > Subscriptions
D. Settings

32. What information can be viewed by clicking on a single subscription in the Office 365 portal?
A. Only the number of licenses in use
B. Only the expiration date for the subscription
C. Only cost per user per year.
D. Cost per user per year, total number of licenses owned and in use, and the expiration date for the subscription

33. Which administrative role in Office 365 has unrestricted access to all features of the tenant?
A. Services Administrator
B. Billing Administrator
C. Global Administrator
D. User Management Administrator

34. Which Office 365 administrative role cannot modify or delete users, groups, and contacts in the tenant?
A. Global Administrator
B. Services Administrator
C. Billing Administrator
D. User Management Administrator

35. What can a User Management Administrator do in Office 365?
A. Only reset user passwords
B. Only assign licenses.
C. Create and delete users, groups, contacts, set user licenses, and reset passwords
D. Modify subscription or billing details

Practice Questions

36. Which administrative role is specifically responsible for viewing and modifying subscription and billing details?
A. Services Administrator
B. Password Administrator
C. Billing Administrator
D. Global Administrator

37. What is the limitation of the Services Administrator role compared to the Global Administrator role?
A. The Services Administrator cannot view service health.
B. The Services Administrator cannot assign licenses or reset passwords.
C. The Services Administrator cannot manage service tickets.
D. The Services Administrator cannot view company information.

38. What is a common term used when discussing Office 365 deployment options, especially regarding Exchange Online, SharePoint Online, and Skype for Business?
A. Multi-factor
B. On-premises
C. Cloud-only
D. Hybrid

39. What should you do before deciding whether to configure a hybrid Office 365 deployment?
A. Begin the installation and configuration processes.
B. Understand what hybrid means.
C. Assign all administrative roles.
D. Purchase additional licenses.

Practice Questions

40. What should administrators make sure of when using WSUS for updates before migrating to Office 365?
A. All updates are declined
B. Only security updates are applied
C. Necessary updates, including Office or Outlook updates, are approved
D. Updates are postponed until after migration

41. What is a key feature of the Exchange hybrid configuration?
A. Single sign-on for Office 365 only
B. A different administrative interface for each environment
C. Cross-premises calendaring
D. Separate mail flow for on-premises and Exchange Online

42. What must be implemented prior to running the Exchange Hybrid Configuration Wizard?
A. Directory synchronization between on-premises and Office 365
B. Active Directory Windows Server 2016 forest-functional level
C. Internet-facing Exchange 2010 CAS/MBX roles
D. A private certificate from a third-party certification authority

43. Which component preserves the Outlook profile and OST file after a mailbox move in Exchange hybrid?
A. Exchange Web Services
B. Mailbox Replication Service
C. Exchange Administrative Center (EAC)
D. Autodiscover service

44. What does SharePoint hybrid one-way outbound topology support?
A. Business Connectivity Services (BCS)
B. Two-stage searches

Practice Questions

C. Search functionality
D. Combined navigation experience

45. What is the purpose of a reverse proxy in the SharePoint hybrid configuration?
A. To manage both environments from a single interface
B. To enable users to traverse links across two environments
C. To provide directory synchronization
D. To separate search results from each environment

46. Which SharePoint hybrid topology supports Business Connectivity Services (BCS)?
A. One-way outbound
B. One-way inbound
C. Two-way hybrid
D. Not supported in any topology

47. How are search results displayed in a SharePoint hybrid environment?
A. In a combined results block
B. As a single, merged list
C. In separate result blocks for each search
D. Alphabetically from both environments

48. What does the Skype hybrid configuration enable for users?
A. Use of Skype for personal calls only
B. Separate SIP addresses for each environment
C. Migration of data like contact lists and scheduled meetings
D. Use of on-premises Lync servers for storage only

Practice Questions

49. In which scenario is an Exchange 2013 (or later) CAS/MBX role required?
A. SharePoint hybrid
B. Skype hybrid
C. Exchange hybrid
D. Office 365 single sign-on

50. What minimum forest-functional level is required for implementing an Exchange hybrid?
A. Windows Server 2000
B. Windows Server 2003
C. Windows Server 2008
D. Windows Server 2012

51. What is the first step in setting up an Office 365 subscription?
A. Assigning administrators
B. Preparing your directories>office>subcription
C. Navigating to https://products.office.com
D. Configuring DNS, firewalls, and proxy servers

52. When choosing a tenant name for Office 365, why is it important to choose carefully?
A. Because it can be easily changed later
B. Because it does not affect the subscription
C. Because it becomes permanent and branded across the subscription
D. Because it is only a temporary placeholder

53. What options are available after selecting a plan on the Office 365 signup page?
A. Free Trial or Buy Now
B. Upgrade or Downgrade

C. Cancel or Postpone
D. Register or Unregister

54. Which role has the right to create other global administrators in Office 365?
A. User Management Administrator
B. Customized Administrator
C. Global Administrator
D. Directory Synchronization Administrator

55. What should you do to add a new administrative account with User administration privileges in Office 365?
A. Modify existing cloud accounts
B. Select Add A User from the Home page or User view
C. Contact each device vendor
D. Update network devices to the latest versions

56. When setting up an administrator role for an Office 365 user account, what should you select in the Roles drop-down menu?
A. Global Administrator
B. Customized Administrator
C. Standard User
D. Guest User

57. What is recommended before deploying Office 365 in terms of network devices?
A. Leaving them as is for compatibility
B. Upgrading them to support Office 365
C. Disconnecting them during setup
D. Replacing them with newer models

Practice Questions

58. What is the purpose of configuring public DNS records for Office 365?
A. To obtain a higher bandwidth for the services
B. To verify domain names and configure necessary records for various services
C. To create a backup of the Office 365 deployment
D. To synchronize on-premises Active Directory with Entra ID

59. What should be done in advance of starting your Office 365 deployment?
A. Creating user accounts
B. Making infrastructure changes required to support Office 365
C. Assigning licenses to users
D. Synchronizing users

60. Where does the Office 365 portal open after setting up a new Office 365 tenant?
A. On the Active Users view
B. On the DNS management page
C. On the tenant's personalized homepage
D. On the page for creating DNS records

61. What is the first step to start the Office 365 portal configuration process for domain name verification?
A. Selecting 'Connect A Domain You Already Own'
B. Clicking the 'Go To Setup' button on the Office 365 Admin Center home page
C. Adding a verification record manually
D. Logging into your GoDaddy account

Practice Questions

62. What should you do if your public DNS is managed internally or hosted by an entity other than GoDaddy?
A. Ignore the TXT record provided for verification
B. Automatically create a TXT record in the domain DNS configuration
C. Select 'Connect A Domain You Already Own'
D. Select 'Add A Verification Record' to manually add the TXT record

63. What happens after you verify your domain ownership with GoDaddy during the setup process?
A. A TXT record is automatically created in the domain DNS configuration
B. You are required to add a TXT record manually
C. You need to log in to your GoDaddy account again
D. You must contact GoDaddy customer support

64. What option should you select if you want Office 365 to configure DNS records for you?
A. Add Records For Me
B. I'll Manage My DNS Records
C. Don't Migrate Email Messages
D. Add A Verification Record

65. When manually updating DNS records for Office 365, which records are necessary?
A. Only MX and TXT records
B. Only A and NS records
C. Exchange Autodiscover, SIP, MX, and CNAME records
D. Only PTR records

66. What should you do if your existing domain name is already configured with certain DNS records for another service?
A. Automatically add new DNS records

Practice Questions

B. Delete the existing DNS records
C. Select the manual configuration options and make the necessary changes
D. Contact Office 365 support for assistance

67. Which type of records are updated to support email functionality in Office 365?
A. A and AAAA records
B. PTR and NS records
C. MX and SPF records
D. SRV and TXT records

68. What is the result of completing the automated Office 365 setup process?
A. Your domain is removed from Office 365
B. Your domain is automatically registered in Office 365
C. You are required to manually configure your email client
D. You can no longer use your domain with other services

69. Which action should be taken after setting up Office 365 to return to the portal home page?
A. Click 'Go To The Admin Center'
B. Log out and log in again
C. Contact Office 365 support
D. Manually configure your DNS settings

70. What functionality is enabled by updating DNS records for Office 365?
A. Only web hosting services
B. Microsoft Outlook and mobile client connectivity and Skype client connectivity

Practice Questions

C. Only instant messaging services
D. Only the ability to send emails

71. What is the Microsoft Entra ID (AAD) Connect tool primarily used for?
A. Managing user licenses manually through the Office 365 portal.
B. Synchronizing user identities between on-premises Active Directory and Microsoft Entra ID.
C. Assigning Microsoft Entra ID groups for the assignment of licenses to users.
D. Creating and managing cloud-only groups directly in Azure.

72. Which event ID indicates that Entra ID has redirected the provisioning endpoint service call to an alternate endpoint?
A. 104
B. 107
C. 115
D. 116

73. Which event ID is associated with the informational message that Entra ID Connect Windows Service (Entra ID Sync) has stopped successfully?
A. 2001
B. 2002
C. 601
D. 650

74. What does the 6110 Warning event indicate in directory synchronization?
A. Full Import Failed
B. Run Profile Step Completed With Errors
C. Configuration has changed since the last run profile
D. Password Synchronization Full Sync Has Started

Practice Questions

75. Which of the following is NOT a valid usage of the Set-MsolUserLicense cmdlet?
A. Assigning a new license SKU to a user.
B. Removing a license from a user.
C. Enabling individual service plans within a license.
D. Assigning a Usage Location to a user.

76. What does event ID 6941 in directory synchronization indicate?
A. Password Synchronization Manager has started.
B. Access to Microsoft Entra ID has been denied.
C. Export encountered one or more specific errors.
D. Server Encryption Keys have been successfully created.

77. What is required for Microsoft Entra ID group-based licensing (GBL)?
A. Microsoft Entra ID Free license
B. Microsoft Entra ID Basic or Premium license
C. MSOnline PowerShell module
D. Entra ID Connect Windows Service to be running

78. Which event ID refers to the informational logging of directory synchronization settings like export threshold and machine name?
A. 116
B. 117
C. 650
D. 651

79. What is the significance of Event ID 601 in password synchronization?
A. Indicates a password sync has started for a management agent.
B. Refers to a batch of password updates to Entra ID having started.
C. Indicates the Password Synchronization Manager has started.
D. Refers to a password change request being successfully transmitted to

Practice Questions

Entra ID.

80. What should be monitored to provide reporting on the standard operation of the Entra ID Connect engine?
A. 6012 - Full Import Failed
B. 6100 - Run Profile Step Completed With Errors
C. 904 - Scheduler-related informational events
D. 6801 - Error Occurred Communicating With Entra ID

81. Which Microsoft 365 service is specifically designed to help organizations detect and respond to threats across their Microsoft 365 environment?

A. Microsoft Defender for Endpoint
B. Microsoft Intune
C. Azure Active Directory
D. Microsoft Forms

82. What type of license is required to use the Entra ID Connect health dashboard?
A. Office 365 E3
B. Entra ID Basic
C. Entra ID Premium
D. Office 365 E5

83. How often do synchronizations typically occur with Entra ID Connect by default?
A. Every 15 minutes
B. Every 30 minutes
C. Hourly
D. Daily

Practice Questions

84. Which feature in the Entra ID Connect health dashboard allows you to export all export errors into a CSV file?
A. Sync Error
B. Notification Settings
C. Export
D. Error Analytics

85. What can you do in the Notification Settings of the Entra ID Connect health dashboard?
A. Change the synchronization frequency
B. Update the Entra ID Premium license
C. Define who should receive notifications from the dashboard
D. View the synchronization error details

86. Which tab would you select in the Entra ID Connect health dashboard to view errors grouped by type?
A. Sync Error By Type
B. Export Error
C. Notification Settings
D. Dashboard Overview

87. How can you identify the object that caused a validation failure in the Entra ID Connect health dashboard?
A. By checking the Pending Export tab
B. By clicking the sync error count
C. By reviewing individual errors in the Synchronization manager
D. By exporting a CSV of the synchronization statistics

88. What is the significant impact of making changes to the Entra ID Connect server configuration?
A. It can change the Entra ID Premium license.

B. It can affect the length of time that synchronization requires and the data synchronized to Entra ID.
C. It will alter the Notification Settings in the dashboard.
D. It will update the synchronization frequency to hourly.

89. What is indicated by an 'object-too-large' error during directory synchronization?
A. The synchronization process is taking too long.
B. The number of attributes on an object is too high.
C. There are too many values in a multivalued attribute.
D. The object has exceeded the storage limit in Entra ID.

90. What should you do if you are not receiving any error emails from the Entra ID Connect synchronization process?
A. Check the Entra ID Connect server's firewall settings.
B. Configure the technical contact for your tenant.
C. Manually synchronize the directories.
D. Reinstall the Entra ID Connect tool.

91. What is the structure of Microsoft Entra ID compared to on-premises Active Directory?
A. Hierarchical with multiple organizational units
B. Flat with no discernable directory structure
C. Single container with organizational boundaries
D. Multiple directories structured by geography

92. Can you have objects with the same value for unique attributes in Microsoft Entra ID?
A. Yes, it is possible and recommended
B. Yes, but it is not recommended

Practice Questions

C. No, Azure does not allow this
D. Only for specific attributes

93. Which attribute must be unique for every object in Entra ID and is used for authentication?
A. SamAccountName
B. ProxyAddresses
C. UserPrincipalName
D. DisplayName

94. Which object types have a UserPrincipalName value in Entra ID?
A. Contacts and groups
B. Only the User object type
C. User and iNetOrgPerson object types
D. All object types

95. What happens if there is a UserPrincipalName conflict during synchronization to Entra ID?
A. The UserPrincipalName is duplicated
B. A new UserPrincipalName is automatically generated
C. The account becomes unusable until resolved
D. Entra ID ignores the conflict.

96. How does the ProxyAddress attribute affect mail flow in Entra ID?
A. It does not affect mail flow at all
B. It is the primary attribute for mail delivery
C. It is used for authentication
D. It can cause mail flow issues if duplicates exist

97. What is the purpose of Duplicate Attribute Resiliency in Entra ID?
A. To allow duplicate attributes

Practice Questions

B. To increase attribute synchronization speed
C. To help remediate attribute value duplication issues
D. To remove the need for unique UserPrincipalNames

98. When was the Duplicate Attribute Resiliency feature introduced in Entra ID?
A. September 2016
B. January 2015
C. December 2017
D. June 2014

99. Which attribute values are commonly conflicted during initial synchronization to Entra ID?
A. DisplayName and SamAccountName
B. UserPrincipalName and ProxyAddresses
C. ObjectGUID and DisplayName
D. SamAccountName and ObjectSID

100. What is the impact of a UserPrincipalName matching a proxy address of an existing Entra ID object?
A. No impact on the existing object
B. The UserPrincipalName is changed automatically
C. Authentication for the new user will be broken
D. The existing object's proxy address is updated

101. What happens when a duplicate UserPrincipalName is synchronized to Entra ID?
A. Entra ID rejects the user.
B. Entra ID deletes the original UserPrincipalName.
C. Entra ID adds a random four-digit number to the UserPrincipalName.
D. Entra ID sends an email notification to the user.

Practice Questions

102. What is the result of attempting to assign an Exchange Online license to a user with a quarantined proxy address?
A. The license is assigned without issues.
B. An error message is displayed.
C. The user's account is deleted.
D. The proxy address is automatically corrected.

103. How is a proxy address conflict handled in Entra ID?
A. The conflicting proxy address is deleted.
B. The user is prompted to change their email address.
C. The duplicate proxy address is quarantined.
D. The user's account is suspended.

104. What does the Duplicate Attribute Resiliency feature do?
A. Prevents any users from being synchronized.
B. Automatically deletes duplicate attributes.
C. Sends repeated notifications about conflicts.
D. Quarantines duplicate attributes without logging an error.

105. Who typically receives the technical notification email from Office 365?
A. The user with the most administrative privileges.
B. The person who created the Office 365 subscription.
C. All users within the organization.
D. External technical support.

106. How can the technical notification email setting be configured?
A. Only through a phone call to Microsoft Support.
B. Through the Office 365 Admin Center portal or using Windows PowerShell.

Practice Questions

C. By sending a request to the Entra ID team.
D. It cannot be changed once set.

107. What is recommended for the technical notification email setting?
A. It should be set to the personal email address of the CEO.
B. It should correspond to a distribution list in the organization.
C. It should be configured to go to a single administrator.
D. It should be disabled for larger organizations.

108. What is the prefix of a UserPrincipalName conflict likely to contain?
A. The user's first and last name.
B. A random eight-digit number.
C. A four-digit number.
D. The word "duplicate."

109. How can you locate error objects in the Office 365 Admin Center portal?
A. By contacting Microsoft Support.
B. By selecting Users With Errors from the Views drop-down list.
C. By manually inspecting each user account.
D. Errors cannot be viewed within the Office 365 Admin Center.

110. What type of email notifications does the Office 365 synchronization process send for UserPrincipalName and proxy address conflicts?
A. Multiple notifications until the issue is resolved.
B. Only a single notification for each conflict.
C. Weekly summary emails.
D. No email notifications are sent for conflicts.

Practice Questions

111. Where can you find detailed information about objects with synchronization errors in Office 365?
A. Users view in the Office 365 Admin Center portal
B. DirSync Status Summary page
C. Windows PowerShell
D. Error resolution email

112. What is the result when Entra ID detects duplicate values during synchronization?
A. It stops the synchronization process.
B. It creates a new object with combined attributes.
C. It removes the conflicting value from the second synchronized object.
D. It sends an alert to the administrator to manually resolve the conflict.

113. What is the purpose of a connector space in directory synchronization?
A. To store real-time updates from the connected data source
B. To maintain a copy of each object and its attributes from the source directory
C. To directly export objects to Entra ID
D. To replace the metaverse as the center of the meta directory universe

114. What is the purpose of the meta directory in Entra ID Connect?
A. To serve as a backup for all directories
B. To synchronize passwords only
C. To maintain and synchronize objects across directories
D. To store metadata about the synchronization process

115. How does Entra ID Connect handle objects it filters out during synchronization?
A. It deletes them from the on-premises Active Directory.
B. It stores them in the Entra ID Connect meta-directory.

Practice Questions

C. It immediately discards them.
D. It archives them in Entra ID.

116. Which Entra ID feature aligns with the special error category 'PropertyConflict' in PowerShell?
A. Identity Protection
B. Access Control
C. Duplicate Attribute Resiliency
D. Multi-Factor Authentication

117. When faced with numerous synchronization errors, what is a recommended approach to manage them?
A. Manually navigate the portal for each error.
B. Use Windows PowerShell to export a sorted list to a CSV file.
C. Ignore the errors as they will resolve on their own.
D. Call Microsoft support for each error.

118. In the context of directory synchronization, what does filtering accomplish?
A. It sorts the objects based on their size.
B. It eliminates objects not wanted in the synchronization.
C. It resolves all synchronization conflicts automatically.
D. It duplicates objects for redundancy purposes.

119. Which of the following is NOT an object type that you would typically filter out during synchronization with Entra ID Connect?
A. Users
B. ForeignSecurityPrincipal objects
C. TPM devices
D. Groups

Practice Questions

120. What is the ultimate goal of the meta directory in Entra ID Connect synchronization?
A. To minimize the storage space used by the directories.
B. To disconnect objects from their original directories.
C. To maintain a connection between each object and its partners for ongoing updates.
D. To create a complex network of directories for security purposes.

121. What is the primary purpose of the Express Installation of Entra ID Connect?
A. To synchronize multiple Active Directory forests
B. To quickly set up Office 365 synchronization with minimal configuration
C. To enable password synchronization without a service account
D. To install SQL Server Express for large environments

122. What must the on-premises Active Directory account provided during Express Installation be a member of?
A. Global Administrators
B. Domain Users
C. Enterprise Administrators
D. Schema Admins

123. What does the On-Premises Directory Synchronization Service Account end with?
A. @yourtenant.onmicrosoft.com
B. @local
C. @admin.onmicrosoft.com
D. @global.onmicrosoft.com

Practice Questions

124. What permissions are granted to the automatically created service account in Active Directory for password synchronization?
A. Read and Write permissions
B. Replicating Directory Changes and Replicating Directory Changes All permissions
C. Full Control permissions
D. Global Administrator permissions

125. What does the Express Installation check regarding the UserPrincipalName suffixes?
A. If they are unique across the forest
B. If they are compliant with password policies
C. If they can be used for authentication with Office 365
D. If they are properly formatted according to Active Directory standards

126. What happens if your environment consists of more than one Active Directory forest?
A. You must use a Global Administrator account for synchronization.
B. You can still use the express installation method.
C. You have to use the custom installation method.
D. Password synchronization is not possible

127. When using Express Installation, what type of account is created in Entra ID tenant?
A. Global Administrator account
B. Standard user account
C. Directory Synchronization account
D. Enterprise Administrator account

128. What is the result if the UserPrincipalName suffix is non-routable, such as .local or .corp?
A. Users can still log on to Office 365 using their UPN.
B. Users will be unable to log on to Office 365 using their UPN.

Practice Questions

C. Users will require a Global Administrator account to log on.
D. The UPN suffix will automatically be converted to a routable domain.

129. What does selecting the Exchange Hybrid Deployment checkbox during Express Installation do?
A. It enables password synchronization only for Exchange attributes.
B. It disables all synchronization features except for those needed for Exchange.
C. It adds additional rules for the writeback of select Exchange-related attributes.
D. It upgrades the Exchange server to support Entra ID Connect.

130. What does the 'Start The Synchronization Process When Configuration Completes' checkbox do during the Express Installation?
A. It initiates a full synchronization of all directories immediately after installation.
B. It schedules the synchronization process to start at a later time.
C. It defers the synchronization until the checkbox is manually selected after installation.
D. It prevents the synchronization process from starting until further notice.

131. What is the difference between the Express and Custom installation of Entra ID Connect?
A. Custom installation does not support SQL Server.
B. Express installation allows for customization of every aspect of the installation.
C. Custom installation allows for specifying a custom installation location for the binaries.
D. Express installation requires a complete re-installation to change configuration options.

Practice Questions

132. Which Microsoft 365 plan is best suited for small to medium-sized businesses that need essential productivity tools and basic security?

A. Microsoft 365 Business Basic
B. Microsoft 365 Enterprise E5
C. Microsoft 365 Business Premium
D. Office 365 E3

133. Which directory is automatically created and should not be deleted after Entra ID Connect installation?
A. C:\AzureADConnect
B. C:\Microsoft Entra ID Sync
C. C:\Program Files\Microsoft Microsoft Entra ID Connect
D. C:\AADSync

134. What is the object limit for Entra ID Connect when using SQL Server Express edition?
A. 10,000 objects
B. 50,000 objects
C. 100,000 objects
D. 500,000 objects

135. What happens if your environment exceeds the recommended number of objects for SQL Server Express with Entra ID Connect?
A. Entra ID Connect will automatically upgrade to a full version of SQL Server.
B. You will need to purchase additional licenses for Entra ID Connect.
C. Entra ID Connect will stop synchronizing additional objects.
D. You must install Entra ID Connect using a full version of SQL Server.

Practice Questions

136. What is the theoretical limit of Entra ID Connect using SQL Server Express based on?
A. Number of user accounts
B. Number of groups and contacts
C. Size of the SQL database
D. Number of domains in the forest

137. What must the logged-on account have when installing Entra ID Connect with an existing SQL Server?
A. Domain Admin rights
B. Local Administrator rights
C. SQL SA permissions
D. Entra ID Connect Operator rights

138. What permissions does the ADSyncAdmins group have?
A. View sync rules and operations run history only
B. Full rights to the Entra ID Connect tool
C. No access to the Sync service console
D. Able to edit but not delete sync rules

139. What happens to the user account used to perform the Entra ID Connect installation after the process completes?
A. It is deleted automatically.
B. It is disabled until reactivated by an administrator.
C. It is placed in the ADSyncOperators group.
D. It is placed in the ADSyncAdmins group.

140. In Custom mode, what must be done prior to installation if specifying custom sync groups for Entra ID Connect?
A. The groups must be associated with the correct SQL Server instance.
B. The groups must be created prior to beginning the installation.

Practice Questions

C. The groups must be populated with all user accounts.
D. The groups must be approved by Microsoft support.

141. What is a prerequisite for using the Password Writeback feature in Entra ID?
A. Entra ID Basic license
B. Entra ID Free license
C. Entra ID Premium P1 or P2 license
D. No specific license is required

142. Which users are supported by the password writeback feature?
A. Cloud-only accounts
B. Federated users using AD FS
C. Synchronized users with Password Sync enabled
D. Both B and C

143. Where do you start the process to enable password reset for the Entra ID tenant?
A. Entra ID Admin Center
B. Office 365 Admin Center
C. Azure Portal Dashboard
D. Office 365 Portal

144. What is the minimum Exchange version required for Group Writeback?
A. Exchange 2010 CU8
B. Exchange 2013 CU8
C. Exchange 2016
D. Exchange 2019

Practice Questions

145. What types of groups are supported by the Group Writeback feature?
A. Security groups
B. Distribution groups
C. Office 365 groups
D. All of the above

146. Which PowerShell module is necessary to enable device writeback in Active Directory?
A. ActiveDirectory
B. AzureAD
C. MSOnline
D. AD FS

147. What is the maximum number of additional attributes that can be synchronized using the Directory Extensions attribute sync?
A. 50
B. 100
C. 150
D. 200

148. For configuring the password reset policy, what is the next step after selecting Authentication Methods in the Entra ID admin portal?
A. Choose the method types allowed
B. Populate the security questions
C. Configure the challenge questions
D. Click Save

149. In which mode does the Entra ID Connect server operate if you want it to read from Active Directory but not export anything to Entra ID?
A. ReadOnly mode
B. Maintenance mode

Practice Questions

C. Staging mode
D. Preview mode

150. What is the outcome when a user successfully enters their challenge information in the password reset portal?
A. They will be asked additional security questions
B. Their password will be changed in the cloud only
C. Their password change will be written back to on-premises Active Directory
D. They will be redirected to the Entra ID admin center

151. What is the purpose of the Configuration Complete page after installing Entra ID Connect?
A. To display advertising for other products
B. To start the synchronization immediately without review
C. To present a summary of the installation status and any environment warnings
D. To uninstall the Entra ID Connect tool

152. Which tool is recommended for backing up the Entra ID Connect configuration for generating HTML reports?
A. Entra ID Connect Configurator
B. Entra ID Connect Synchronization Service Manager
C. Entra ID Connect Health Agent
D. Entra ID Connect Configuration Documenter

153. What does the precedence value in Entra ID Connect synchronization rules indicate?
A. The sequential order in which rules are written
B. The numerical value that indicates the order of importance of the rules

Practice Questions

C. The number of objects the rule applies to
D. The time interval at which the rule runs

154. What type of synchronization rule would you create to force a different attribute value than what is set by existing rules?
A. A rule with a higher numerical precedence value
B. An inbound rule with the same precedence value
C. A rule with a lower numerical precedence value
D. An outbound rule with any precedence value

155. What happens if two objects from different forests are configured to join on attributes such as Mail?
A. The order they were added to Entra ID Connect affects the resulting objects synchronized to Entra ID.
B. They are automatically assigned the same precedence value.
C. The objects will not join and will cause an error.
D. The attributes from the forest with a lower numeric precedence will take priority.

156. If you want to ensure a specific value from a particular forest takes precedence during synchronization, what should you do?
A. Clone the forest
B. Remove the existing synchronization rules
C. Clone the synchronization rule(s) that flow those attributes as a higher precedence
D. Increase the numerical value of the existing synchronization rule

157. Which PowerShell command initiates the synchronization process immediately in Entra ID Connect?
A. Start-ADSyncSyncCycle
B. Enable-ADSyncScheduler

Practice Questions

C. Initiate-ADSyncNow
D. Trigger-ADSyncProcess

158. What is the role of the Entra ID Connect staging mode?
A. It is used for initial data population only.
B. It serves as a warm-standby server for failover purposes.
C. It permanently disables object synchronization.
D. It is a mode for uninstalling Entra ID Connect.

159. What should be done if you have data in your on-premises Active Directory that should not leave your organization?
A. Enable staging mode
B. Use the Azure App and Attribute filtering option to remove the attribute
C. Ignore the data during synchronization
D. Manually delete the data from Entra ID after synchronization

160. Upon completing your configuration review in staging mode, how do you export data to Entra ID?
A. Run the Entra ID Connect Configuration Documenter
B. Disable staging mode and enable the synchronization scheduler
C. Manually copy the data to Entra ID
D. Restart the Entra ID Connect server

161. What is the synchronization frequency of user password changes from on-premises Active Directory to Office 365 with Entra ID Connect?
A. Every 30 minutes
B. Every 1 to 2 minutes
C. Every 5 minutes
D. Once daily

Practice Questions

162. How are passwords protected during synchronization to Office 365?
A. They are transmitted in clear text.
B. They are hashed with SHA-256.
C. They are encrypted with an MD5 key and salt.
D. They are only protected by an HTTPS session

163. Which permissions are automatically delegated to the service account in express mode during Entra ID Connect installation?
A. Replicating Directory Changes and Replicating Directory Changes In Filtered Set
B. Replicating Directory Changes and Replicating Directory Changes All
C. Write and Read permissions on all user objects
D. Administrative rights on the Entra ID Connect server

164. How does pass-through authentication differ from password synchronization in Entra ID Connect?
A. Pass-through authentication redirects authentication requests to an on-premises server.
B. Pass-through authentication processes authentication requests in Microsoft Entra ID.
C. Pass-through authentication does not require any on-premises components.
D. Pass-through authentication allows on-premises Active Directory to process authentication requests without transmitting passwords.

165. What are the server requirements for deploying the pass-through authentication processing agent?
A. Windows Server 2008 or later
B. Windows Server 2012 or later
C. Windows Server 2012R2 or later
D. Windows Server 2016 or later

Practice Questions

166. What is the result when on-premises Active Directory passwords are set to expire and password synchronization is used?
A. The user will be prompted to change their password immediately in Office 365.
B. The user's cloud account password is set to Never Expire.
C. The user cannot log in to Office 365 until the password is updated on-premises.
D. Password expiration is synchronized and enforced by Office 365.

167. What is required for a multi-forest configuration to support pass-through authentication?
A. A one-way trust between the forests
B. A two-way trust between the forests
C. Separate Entra ID Connect servers for each forest
D. A forest trust between the forests

168. What UserPrincipalName value is required for synchronization to Office 365 with pass-through authentication?
A. Any on-premises Active Directory UserPrincipalName value
B. The email attribute value from on-premises Active Directory
C. The value from the on-premises Active Directory UserPrincipalName attribute that is a routable UPN suffix
D. Any unique identifier assigned by the Entra ID Connect tool

169. Which additional installations are required when selecting Federation with AD FS during the Entra ID Connect setup?
A. Active Directory Rights Management Services and DNS Server
B. Domain Controller and Certificate Authority
C. AD FS Federation server role and Web Application Proxy server role
D. DHCP Server and Network Policy Server

Practice Questions

170. What type of authentication method can be selected if company policies prohibit the transmission of passwords over the public Internet?
A. Password Synchronization
B. Pass-through Authentication
C. Federation with AD FS
D. Single Sign-On (SSO)

171. What format is required for entering forest user name credentials in the Entra ID Connect installation wizard?
A. UPN format (e.g., user@domain.com)
B. Email format (e.g., user@domain.com)
C. DOMAIN\UserName format
D. Plain username without domain

172. What happens if you provide credentials in the UPN format during the Entra ID Connect setup?
A. The installation proceeds with a warning.
B. The installation wizard exits, and you have to start over.
C. The UPN is converted to DOMAIN\UserName format automatically.
D. The credentials are accepted, but synchronization will fail.

173. What minimum group membership is required for the service account used by Entra ID Connect?
A. Domain Administrators
B. Domain Users
C. Enterprise Admins
D. Schema Admins

174. Where can you find the additional permissions required for features such as Group Writeback in Entra ID Connect?
A. In the Entra ID Connect installation manual

Practice Questions

B. On the Microsoft official website
C. In the Entra ID Connect wizard
D. In the Entra ID Connect troubleshooting guide

175. What determines the order of synchronization rules in Entra ID Connect?
A. The alphabetical order of the directory names
B. The size of each directory
C. The order in which directories are added during setup
D. The number of users in each directory

176. What should you do if you encounter unverified domain suffixes during the Entra ID Connect installation?
A. Stop the installation immediately.
B. Ignore the warning and proceed.
C. Manually verify the domain suffixes before proceeding.
D. Contact Microsoft support for assistance.

177. What is the default attribute used for the UserPrincipalName value in Entra ID?
A. SAM Account Name
B. Email
C. UserPrincipalName from on-premises AD schema
D. Common Name (CN)

178. Which attribute is commonly used as an alternate for the UserPrincipalName in Entra ID?
A. Mail
B. DisplayName
C. ObjectGUID

D. sAMAccountName

179. What is the consequence of selecting the wrong UserPrincipalName attribute during the Entra ID Connect setup?
A. You can change it later with a simple configuration update.
B. You must uninstall and reinstall Entra ID Connect.
C. It will automatically correct itself over time.
D. It has no significant impact on the installation.

180. What does a gray check box with a check mark indicate in the Domain and OU filtering page of Entra ID Connect?
A. The OU is included, and new sub-OUs will be automatically excluded.
B. The OU is included, and any new sub-OUs added will be automatically included.
C. The OU and all sub-OUs will be excluded from synchronization.
D. The OU is excluded from synchronization, but sub-OUs are included.

181. What is the consequence of failing to select the correct user-matching option in a multi-forest Entra ID Connect setup?
A. No impact on the synchronization process
B. Automatic correction by Entra ID Connect
C. A reinstallation of the Entra ID Connect tool is required
D. Users will be granted admin privileges

182. Which attribute is critical for the synchronization of Exchange mailbox objects to Office 365 in Entra ID Connect?
A. UserPrincipalName
B. ObjectSID
C. sAMAccountName
D. mailNickname

Practice Questions

183. What does the msExchMasterAccountSID attribute contain?
A. The security identifier of the mailbox in the resource forest
B. The unique identifier of the mailbox in the account forest
C. The security identifier of the user account from the account forest
D. The GUID of the user's Exchange Server

184. In an Exchange resource forest scenario, how are the user objects in the two forests typically configured?
A. Both user and mailbox accounts are enabled
B. The user account is enabled, and the mailbox account is disabled
C. Both user and mailbox accounts are disabled.
D. The user account is disabled, and the mailbox account is enabled

185. What is the expected configuration for the msExchRecipientTypeDetails attribute for a linked mailbox?
A. It must be set to a value of 1
B. It must be set to a value of 2
C. It must be cleared (no value)
D. It must be set to any value other than 2

186. When using the Mail Attribute for user joins in Entra ID Connect, what scenario is this configuration most commonly used for?
A. When there's a single directory with Exchange mailboxes
B. When using a third-party directory synchronization tool
C. When performing global address list synchronization between forests
D. When all users have unique sAMAccountNames

187. When Entra ID Connect performs user joins using sAMAccountName and mailNickname, what is expected of these attributes?
A. They can be duplicated across forests
B. They are not required to be unique

Practice Questions

C. They must be unique within their forests
D. They must be populated for all users

188. What will happen if you manually select an attribute that is not in the Entra ID Connect metaverse for user joins?
A. The installation will proceed without errors
B. Entra ID Connect will automatically correct the configuration
C. The installation will fail with an error
D. Entra ID Connect will default to another attribute

189. What is the role of the SourceAnchor attribute in Entra ID Connect?
A. It is used to join user objects across forests
B. It uniquely identifies an object and anchors it to the source object in on-premises directories
C. It is the primary attribute used for user authentication
D. It is a temporary identifier that changes frequently

190. What should be considered when selecting an alternate attribute for SourceAnchor in Entra ID Connect?
A. The attribute should be easily changeable
B. The attribute should be a multi-valued Active Directory attribute
C. The attribute should never change
D. The attribute should be based on mutable user data

191. What is the purpose of the 'Sway' feature in Office 365?
A. To configure security settings
B. To manage tasks and synchronize with Exchange
C. To generate and import content to create stories
D. To add new domains to the organization

Practice Questions

192. How can Sways be shared?
A. Publicly only
B. With organization users only
C. Both publicly and with organization users
D. Neither publicly nor with organization users

193. How is access to Sway configured for a user?
A. By setting a password policy
B. By enabling or disabling guest access
C. By assigning or removing their Sway license
D. By customizing the help desk information

194. What is Microsoft To-Do?
A. A security feature in Office 365
B. A data migration service
C. A task management app
D. A domain management tool

195. How can an admin configure the password policy for managed accounts?
A. By editing the Organization Profile
B. By modifying the Release Preferences
C. By selecting Edit in the Password Policy section
D. By adding a custom tile

196. Which feature requires an additional license to enable self-service password reset?
A. Sway
B. SharePoint
C. Entra ID Premium
D. Office 365 Groups

Copyright © 2024 VERSAtile Reads. All rights reserved.
This material is protected by copyright, any infringement will be dealt with legal and punitive action.

Practice Questions

197. What can you NOT change after creating your Office 365 tenant?
A. The organization's name and address
B. The custom themes for your organization
C. The data center regions where your data is located
D. The Release Preferences setting

198. What can be customized in the Office 365 portal to match an organization's branding?
A. The password policy
B. The data migration tools
C. The custom themes
D. The security & privacy settings

199. Where can you add a partner of record or subscription advisor for your Office 365 subscriptions?
A. Under Security & Compliance
B. In the Usage reports
C. Under Billing | Subscriptions
D. In the Domains settings

200. How do you add a new custom tile to the App Launcher for each user?
A. By enabling mailbox auditing in Exchange Online
B. By clicking the +Add A Custom Tile button
C. By modifying the Release Preferences setting
D. By configuring new domains

201. What does a notification classified as "Plan for Change" in the Message Center indicate?
A. A new feature will be available soon.
B. A change is coming in how to deploy or manage a feature.

Practice Questions

C. An existing issue like duplicate proxy addresses needs to be fixed.
D. Monthly update summaries are provided.

202. Where can the Exchange Admin Center be accessed from within the Office 365 Admin Center?
A. Under the Security & Compliance Center
B. Within the Service Health page
C. From the Service admin centers
D. Through the Message Center page

203. What is the purpose of the Compliance Management section in the Exchange Admin Center?
A. To manage user and shared mailboxes, groups, resources, and contacts.
B. To configure domain relationships and add-ins for Exchange Online.
C. To create and manage retention policies, run auditing reports, and configure journaling.
D. To control malware and spam filtering settings.

204. What can be configured in the Mail Flow settings of the Exchange Admin Center?
A. Accepted domains and transport rules.
B. Public folder hierarchies.
C. Unified messaging dial plans.
D. Mobile device access policies.

205. Which admin center would you use to manage user profiles and organization properties for SharePoint Online?
A. Exchange Admin Center
B. Skype for Business Admin Center
C. SharePoint Admin Center
D. Office 365 Admin Center

Practice Questions

206. How does Command Logging in the Exchange Admin Center assist administrators?
A. By providing real-time system health monitoring.
B. By showing Windows PowerShell commands that correspond to actions taken in the admin center.
C. By enabling automated script execution for repetitive tasks.
D. By offering a direct link to the Office 365 Hybrid Configuration Wizard.

207. What is the primary function of the "Hybrid" section in the Exchange Admin Center?
A. To start the Office 365 Hybrid Configuration Wizard.
B. To manage on-premises Exchange integration.
C. To configure malware protection options.
D. To set up public folder mailboxes.

208. What is the purpose of the "Users" menu in the Skype for Business Admin Center?
A. To configure tenant-wide Skype for Business settings.
B. To manage individual user settings, such as audio or video features.
C. To specify global settings for meeting invites.
D. To manage downloadable and online troubleshooting tools.

209. Which SharePoint Online setting allows the management of term sets for use in the tenant?
A. BCS
B. Term Store
C. Device Access
D. User Profiles

Practice Questions

210. Where in the Office 365 Admin Center can you find an overview of the current service status and incidents affecting your tenant?
A. The Message Center
B. The Service Health page
C. The Compliance Management section
D. The Exchange Admin Center

211. Which attribute can be used as a SourceAnchor that is unique for every object and is suitable for companies with mature Identity Management systems?
A. Social Security Number
B. EmployeeID
C. ObjectGUID
D. Proxy Addresses

212. What should an organization consider before using PII for SourceAnchor synchronization to Office 365?
A. Ensuring attribute uniqueness
B. Getting approval from the IT department
C. Consulting legal and corporate security teams
D. Converting to base64 encoding

213. What is one of the main reasons organizations might select an alternate SourceAnchor instead of ObjectGUID?
A. To improve security
B. Because of mergers and acquisitions
C. To simplify the IT infrastructure
D. To comply with PII regulations

Practice Questions

214. During the Entra ID Connect installation, what does selecting a group for filtering accomplish?
A. Synchronizes all users in the organization
B. Filters out specific attributes from synchronization
C. Enables synchronization of only the objects in the selected group
D. Automatically includes nested groups for synchronization

215. What must a group used for filtering reside in to function properly?
A. A top-level OU within the scope of the solution
B. The default User container
C. Any shared network folder
D. A global security group

216. Which feature of Entra ID Connect writes back certain attributes from Exchange Online to on-premises Active Directory?
A. Password Writeback
B. Exchange Hybrid Deployment
C. Password Synchronization
D. Entra ID App and Attribute Filtering

217. What type of additional subscriptions may be required for certain Optional Features in Entra ID Connect?
A. Office 365 subscriptions
B. Entra ID Premium licensing
C. Active Directory licenses
D. Exchange Online Protection licenses

218. What is the main purpose of the Entra ID App and Attribute Filtering feature in Entra ID Connect?
A. To install additional applications
B. To synchronize every attribute available

Practice Questions

C. To tailor synchronization to specific workloads or exclude attributes
D. To configure password policies for Entra ID

219. What happens if you clear an application checkbox in the Entra ID Apps filtering?
A. It adds the application to the synchronization process.
B. It removes all outbound rules related to that application, stopping synchronization.
C. It resets the application to default settings.
D. It synchronizes the application immediately

220. What feature allows users to change their password in Entra ID and have it updated in the on-premises Active Directory?
A. Password Synchronization
B. Password Writeback
C. AD FS
D. Pass-through authentication

221. What role is needed to reset passwords, manage service requests, and monitor Office 365 service health?
A. Global admin
B. Billing admin
C. User management admin
D. Password admin

222. Which type of user account is typically unable to sign in to Office 365 when Directory Synchronization is enabled?
A. Unlicensed users
B. Users with errors
C. Sign-In blocked users

Practice Questions

D. Guest users

223. Where can you find the option to create a custom view for filtering users in the Office 365 Admin Center?
A. Data Migration
B. Add Custom View
C. Deleted Users
D. Groups

224. Who can create shared contacts in the Office 365 Admin Center?
A. Any user with an Office 365 account
B. Only global admins
C. Global admins and Exchange admins
D. Service admins

225. Which page shows external users who are members of Office 365 groups?
A. Users with errors
B. Contacts
C. Guest users
D. Deleted users

226. For how many days can deleted users be restored after removal in Office 365?
A. 7 days
B. 15 days
C. 30 days
D. 60 days

227. What are room and equipment mailboxes in Exchange Online?
A. Regular user mailboxes

Practice Questions

B. Special types of shared mailboxes
C. External user accounts
D. Public website templates

228. Through which page can you perform basic site operations for SharePoint Online in Office 365?
A. Groups
B. Shared Mailboxes
C. Rooms & Equipment
D. Sites

229. What can Billing admins do in Office 365?
A. Reset passwords for any user
B. Make purchases and manage subscriptions
C. Create contacts and shared mailboxes
D. Configure sharing settings for SharePoint sites

230. Which groups can only be created and managed in Office 365?
A. Shared mailboxes
B. Office 365 groups
C. Distribution lists
D. Contacts

231. Where can you add a partner of record in the Office 365 admin center?
A. Purchase Services page
B. Services & Add-Ins page
C. Subscriptions page
D. Support page

Practice Questions

232. What is the first step to signing in to Office 365 with an account authorized to make service changes?
A. Select the App Launcher icon and then click Admin.
B. Select the Support menu.
C. Go to the Services & Add-Ins page.
D. Navigate to Billing and select Subscriptions.

233. Which page displays a list of purchased subscriptions or SKUs in Office 365?
A. Licenses page
B. Purchase Services page
C. Bills page
D. Subscriptions page

234. How can you manage Calendar sharing permissions for the Exchange Online organization?
A. Through Azure Multi-Factor Authentication
B. By accessing the Calendar service configuration item
C. Via the Support menu
D. Through the Licenses page

235. What is required to enable Cortana to search Office 365 content on Windows 10 devices?
A. Configure Cortana on the Services & Add-Ins page.
B. Enable Cortana services on the Cortana service setting.
C. Integration with Azure Multi-Factor Authentication.
D. Directory Synchronization settings must be configured

236. What can you do on the Licenses page under Billing?
A. Purchase additional licenses
B. View a high-level snapshot of available licenses

Practice Questions

C. Assign licenses to new users

D. Request a refund for unused licenses

237. Where do you go to purchase additional services for your Office 365 tenant?

A. Bills page

B. Subscriptions page

C. Purchase Services page

D. Services & Add-Ins page

238. To whom are Billing notifications sent by default?

A. Every user in the tenant

B. Designated finance officers only

C. Global administrators and billing administrators

D. The partner of record

239. How do you upload an add-in from the Office Store to your Office 365 tenant?

A. Through the Support menu

B. By going to the Purchase Services page

C. On the Services & Add-Ins page

D. From the Subscriptions page

240. What is the purpose of Azure MultiFactor Authentication in Office 365?

A. To manage licenses

B. To manage Calendar sharing permissions

C. To control how users access your tenant

D. To send billing notifications to administrators

Practice Questions

241. What happens when a user tries to sign into Docs.com with their Office 365 ID if the service has not been enabled for their organization?
A. The user can still access Docs.com without any issues.
B. The user receives a confirmation email to enable access.
C. The user is redirected to the Office 365 dashboard.
D. The user sees an error stating that the service has been turned off for their organization

242. When did Docs.com stop allowing users to upload new content?
A. June 19, 2017
B. December 15, 2017
C. August 1, 2017
D. It still allows uploads

243. What types of data does GigJam support for integration?
A. Calendars, contacts, email, opportunities, accounts, and files
B. Photos, music, videos, chat histories, and bookmarks
C. Spreadsheets, databases, presentations, and drawings
D. Health records, legal documents, and government IDs

244. Are Integrated Apps enabled or disabled by default in Office 365?
A. Enabled
B. Disabled
C. Not available in Office 365
D. Available only on demand

245. What is the purpose of the Azure Information Protection service?
A. To provide cloud storage solutions
B. To sign, encrypt, and manage content
C. To enhance collaboration through chat and video

Practice Questions

D. To manage external sharing options for SharePoint

246. Which license is required to use Microsoft Teams?
A. SharePoint License
B. Separate user license
C. Azure Information Protection License
D. GigJam License

247. What can be managed from the Office 365 Groups settings page?
A. External membership and access to content
B. Internal reporting structures
C. Group chat and file-sharing permissions
D. Office software download settings

248. By default, is Office Online configured to work with third-party storage services?
A. Yes
B. No
C. Only with OneDrive
D. Only with Google Drive

249. What is the main focus of StaffHub?
A. To provide a chat-based collaboration hub
B. To enable content creation and sharing
C. To serve desk-less workers in service industries
D. To manage emails and calendars

250. What does enabling self-provisioning in StaffHub allow users to do?
A. Schedule meetings with audio and video
B. Create their accounts using the application interface

Practice Questions

C. Access the Office Store and download apps

D. Encrypt and manage content

251. What PowerShell endpoint would you use to manage Exchange Online Protection?

A. https://outlook.office365.com/powerhshell-liveid

B. https://ps.compliance.protection.outlook.com/powershell-liveid

C. https://ps.protection.outlook.com/powershell-liveid

D. https://office365.cloudappsecurity.com

252. Which role enables users to manage retention policies?

A. Compliance Administrator

B. Retention Management

C. Audit Logs

D. Device Management

253. If you want to grant a user the ability to run and export audit reports, which role should they be assigned?

A. Security Administrator

B. Organization Configuration

C. Audit Logs

D. Role Management

254. Which URL do you use to access the Security & Compliance Center PowerShell endpoint?

A. https://ps.compliance.protection.outlook.com/powershell-liveid

B. https://ps.protection.outlook.com/powershell-liveid

C. https://outlook.office365.com/powerhshell-liveid

D. https://office365.cloudappsecurity.com

Practice Questions

255. Which role should be assigned to a user who needs to edit settings and reports for device management features?
A. Compliance Administrator
B. Device Management
C. DLP Compliance Management
D. Security Administrator

256. What should you do if you want to manage advanced alerts in Office 365?
A. Enable Advanced Security Management
B. Assign the Manage Alerts role
C. Use the New Alert Policy Wizard
D. Import the Advanced Alerts module via PowerShell

257. Which role gives users the ability to search mailboxes and get an estimate of search results but requires additional roles to preview or export them?
A. Compliance Search
B. Hold
C. Export
D. Preview

258. What happens to the content when it is placed 'on hold' in the Office 365 Security & Compliance Center?
A. It is immediately deleted.
B. It is stored in a secure location and cannot be modified or deleted by content owners.
C. It is stored in a secure location, but content owners can modify or delete the original content.
D. It becomes encrypted and unreadable to anyone except the global administrator

Practice Questions

259. Which role would you assign to a user who needs to decrypt RMS-encrypted email messages when exporting search results?
A. RMS Decrypt
B. Export
C. Compliance Administrator
D. Security Administrator

260. Which Security & Compliance Center feature is accessed by users with the 'Case Management' role?
A. Advanced Threat Management
B. Data Loss Prevention Policies
C. eDiscovery Cases
D. Advanced Security Management

261. What subscription do you need to access the Alerts Dashboard with the option to configure analytics?
A. Office 365 A1
B. Office 365 E3
C. Office 365 E5
D. Office 365 Business Premium

262. Where can you enable Office 365 Analytics within the Security & Compliance Center?
A. Threat Management
B. Threat Explorer
C. Alerts Dashboard
D. Compliance Management

Practice Questions

263. Which feature replaces View Security Alerts if you have licenses that include Advanced Security Management?
A. View Threat Alerts
B. Manage Alerts
C. View Alerts
D. Audit Log Search

264. What must you do to start generating activity alerts in the Security & Compliance Center?
A. Enable Threat Management
B. Start Recording User And Admin Activities
C. Enable Compliance Management
D. Configure Alert Policies

265. Where can you find the option to configure Advanced Alerts and Alert Policies in Office 365?
A. Alerts | Dashboard
B. Alerts | Manage Alerts
C. Security & Compliance Center | Threat Management
D. Security & Compliance Center | Data Loss Prevention

266. What PowerShell cmdlet is used to enable mailbox auditing for all mailboxes in Exchange Online?
A. Enable-MailboxAuditing
B. Set-Mailbox -AuditEnabled $true
C. Get-Mailbox -ResultSize Unlimited | Set-Mailbox -AuditEnabled $true
D. Set-AuditConfig -EnableMailboxAuditing $true

267. After enabling the recording of user and admin activities, what must you confirm by clicking 'Turn On'?
A. Threat Management

Practice Questions

B. Security Auditing
C. Compliance Management
D. Data Loss Prevention

268. What action might trigger a dialog box that is the same as running Enable-OrganizationCustomization from Windows PowerShell?
A. Turning on Threat Management
B. Enabling Security Auditing
C. Updating organization settings
D. Creating a new alert policy

269. When creating a new alert policy, where can you select the specific events that you want to audit?
A. Under 'Send This Alert To'
B. Under 'Activities'
C. In 'Alert Recipients'
D. Under 'Manage Alerts'

270. Which PowerShell cmdlets can you use to manage activity alerts when connected to the Security & Compliance Center PowerShell endpoint?
A. New-CompliancePolicy and Set-CompliancePolicy
B. New-ThreatPolicy and Set-ThreatPolicy
C. New-ActivityAlert and Set-ActivityAlert
D. New-SecurityPolicy and Set-SecurityPolicy

271. What is the main function of a user with the Security Reader role in the Office 365 Security & Compliance Center?
A. Manage alert policies and threat management
B. Create and manage eDiscovery cases
C. Read-only access to several security features
D. Assign permissions to other users

Practice Questions

272. Which role should be assigned to a user who needs to view and export audit reports in the Office 365 Security & Compliance Center?
A. Security Administrator
B. Reviewer
C. View-Only Audit Logs
D. Global Administrator

273. What can eDiscovery Administrators do that eDiscovery Managers cannot?
A. Add and remove members to a case
B. Place content locations on hold
C. Manage any eDiscovery case without being a member
D. View and open the list of eDiscovery cases they are members of

274. Which role is capable of accessing and managing the Service Assurance section in the Office 365 Security & Compliance Center?
A. Security Reader
B. Service Assurance User
C. Compliance Administrator
D. Organization Management

275. What must a user do to search the Exchange audit logs?
A. Assign the Security Administrator role
B. Enable Office 365 Analytics
C. Assign the permissions in Exchange Online
D. Use the Threat Explorer feature

276. Which role group in the Security & Compliance Center has two subgroups, namely eDiscovery Manager and eDiscovery Administrator?
A. Compliance Administrator

Practice Questions

B. Organization Management
C. eDiscovery Manager
D. Security Administrator

277. What primary action can members of the 'Reviewer' role perform in the eDiscovery context?
A. Create and modify eDiscovery cases
B. View cases they are members of and have been granted access to
C. Export search results
D. Add themselves to any eDiscovery case

278. What feature allows users to analyze threats in the Office 365 environment, displaying attacks over time and by threat families?
A. Threat Management Dashboard
B. Threat Explorer
C. Incidents Dashboard
D. Service Assurance Dashboard

279. Which role is required to create and define supervision policies?
A. Supervisory Review Administrator
B. Compliance Administrator
C. eDiscovery Administrator
D. Service Assurance User

280. What is the purpose of the Incidents feature within Threat Management?
 A. To manage settings for device management and data loss prevention
 B. To track activities and manage ongoing threat investigations
 C. To assign permissions to other users in the organization
 D. To provide read-only access to threat management configurations

Practice Questions

281. Which Office applications currently do not support Safe Links?
A. Office Online
B. Office for Mac
C. Office for iOS
D. All of the above

282. What must a user have for Safe Links to work?
A. Office 365 subscription
B. Advanced Threat Protection license
C. Security & Compliance Center access
D. Quarantine access

283. Where can you review items in quarantine in the Security & Compliance Center?
A. Threat Management | Dashboard
B. Threat Management | Quarantine
C. Service Assurance | Dashboard
D. Reports | Manage Schedules

284. What types of messages can be filtered on the Quarantine page?
A. Bulk, Spam, Transport Rule, Phish
B. Malware, High confidence spam, System
C. Unwanted software, Hacked accounts
D. Spoofed senders, Encryption

285. The Advanced Threats page in the Security & Compliance Center is accessible to users with which type of license?
A. Office 365 E3
B. Advanced Threat Protection
C. Enterprise Mobility + Security E5
D. Microsoft 365 Business

Practice Questions

286. Where can you manage the schedules for reports in the Security & Compliance Center?
A. Reports | Dashboard
B. Reports | Manage Schedules
C. Service Assurance | Settings
D. Advanced Threats | Threat Protection Status

287. What type of documents can you find under the Trust documents section in the Security & Compliance Center?
A. Quarantine reports
B. Scheduled reports
C. Service assurance documents
D. Compliance regulations documents

288. What can you select on the Service Assurance | Settings page?
A. Report schedules
B. Advanced Threat Protection settings
C. Types of assurance documents based on your region and industry
D. Quarantine message types

289. Which section would you visit to download certification reports available for Office 365?
A. Compliance Reports
B. Audited Controls
C. Trust Documents
D. Advanced Threats

290. What is displayed on the Audited Controls page?
A. Scheduled reports
B. Data protection and privacy controls
C. User permissions and roles

Practice Questions

D. Standards Office 365 services have been audited against

291. What is the primary purpose of classifications in the context of data governance in Office 365?
A. To change user permissions
B. To install software updates
C. To manage the life cycle of information
D. To create new user accounts

292. In Office 365, how are labels used?
A. To categorize or classify information
B. To encrypt emails and documents
C. To create new user profiles
D. To organize calendar events

293. Which feature takes precedence: retention or deletion?
A. Deletion
B. Retention
C. Neither do they have equal precedence
D. The feature set first by the admin

294. If conflicting retention policies are applied to content, which policy prevails?
A. The policy with the shortest retention period
B. The policy applied most recently
C. The policy with the longest retention period
D. The policy with the most conditions

295. Which action prevails when content is subject to multiple policies that delete content?
A. The action with the longest deletion period

Practice Questions

B. The action with the shortest deletion period
C. The action specified in the most specific policy
D. The action specified by the global administrator

296. What happens if a user manually applies a label to content in Office 365?
A. The label can't be changed or removed by the user
B. An auto-apply label can replace the manual label
C. The label can be changed or removed by the user
D. The content is immediately archived

297. What is the result when multiple auto-apply label policies conflict?
A. The label with the shortest retention period is used
B. No label is applied
C. The label for the oldest rule is assigned
D. The labels are merged into a composite label

298. Which types of content can labels be automatically applied to based on sensitive information types?
A. Exchange Online public folders
B. Skype data
C. SharePoint and OneDrive content
D. All Office 365 services and features

299. When creating a label in the Security & Compliance Center, what can be configured in relation to content retention?
A. Only the retention period
B. Only the deletion action
C. Both the retention period and the deletion action
D. The encryption level

Practice Questions

300. What must be created to publish a label for manual application?
A. A label policy
B. A new user group
C. A DLP transport rule
D. A SharePoint site

301. What type of license is required to apply retention policies to Exchange Online content?
A. Exchange Online Plan 1
B. Exchange Online Plan 2
C. Office 365 E3
D. Exchange Online Plan 1 with the Exchange Online Archiving add-on license

302. Where is a copy of the content retained when a user edits or deletes content that's covered by a retention policy in SharePoint?
A. In the Recycle Bin
B. In the user's folder
C. In the Preservation Hold library
D. In the site collection administrator's mailbox

303. How long is content kept in the Recoverable Items folder by default before it is purged?
A. 7 days
B. 14 days
C. 30 days
D. 93 days

304. What happens to the contents of an inactive mailbox in Exchange Online?

Practice Questions

A. They are immediately deleted
B. They are retained indefinitely
C. They are subject to the retention policy that was in place before the mailbox became inactive
D. They are moved to the site collection administrator's mailbox

305. If you need to preserve content for a minimum of 3 years from when it was created, which option should you select when creating a retention policy?
A. Delete after 3 years
B. Retain for 3 years and then delete
C. Retain indefinitely
D. Retain for 5 years

306. What is the Preservation Lock feature used for?
A. To extend the retention period
B. To ensure retention policies can be modified at any time
C. To comply with SEC Rule 17a-4 by preventing policy removal or modification
D. To lock content so that it cannot be edited or deleted

307. What happens to content in SharePoint not modified or deleted during the retention period?
A. It remains in the original location indefinitely
B. It is moved to the site collection administrator's mailbox
C. It is moved to the first-stage Recycle Bin
D. It is archived in the Preservation Hold library

308. How long is the total retention period for documents that span both the first-stage and second-stage Recycle Bins in SharePoint?
A. 14 days
B. 30 days

C. 93 days
D. 5 years

309. When should you use retention policies over labels in Office 365?
A. When you need to apply retention policies automatically to all content types in Office 365
B. When you want users to categorize data in Outlook, OneDrive, or SharePoint
C. When you want to categorize data automatically
D. When you want to apply labels to Exchange Online public folders

310. What is the main purpose of setting up a supervision policy in Office 365?
A. To automatically delete content that violates company policies
B. To capture employee communications for examination by reviewers
C. To lock content for compliance with SEC Rule 17a-4
D. To prevent users from deleting their emails

311. Which cmdlet can be used to verify the permissions on a folder named for a policy configured under Supervision in the Security & Compliance Center?
A. Set-MailboxPermission
B. Get-MailboxFolderPermission
C. Set-MailboxFolderPermission
D. New-ComplianceSecurityFilter

312. What is the result of creating a supervision policy in the Security & Compliance Center?
A. A new SupervisoryReview{guid} mailbox is created.

Practice Questions

B. A new Compliance Management role group is created.

C. A new set of transport rules is created.

D. A new content search is initiated.

313. When adding a SupervisoryReview mailbox to a user's Outlook profile, what type of server should be selected in the Add Account Wizard?
A. POP3
B. IMAP
C. Office 365
D. Exchange ActiveSync

314. What should be done if you need to re-hide the SupervisoryReview mailbox from the global address list after adding it to reviewers' profiles?
A. Delete the mailbox.
B. Remove all permissions.
C. Re-hide it from the global address list.
D. Create a new SupervisoryReview mailbox

315. What must be enabled in order to perform an Audit Log Search for user activity in Exchange Online?
A. eDiscovery Manager role
B. Exchange mailbox audit logging
C. Advanced Security Management licensing
D. Reviewer role

316. What is the purpose of the New-ComplianceSecurityFilter cmdlet?
A. To enable audit log search
B. To assign permissions to OneDrive for Business sites
C. To limit the scope of whom eDiscovery managers can search
D. To create a new supervision policy

Practice Questions

317. In what scenario can the command 'New-ComplianceSecurityFilter' be useful?
A. When exporting search results
B. When granting eDiscovery permissions
C. When limiting an eDiscovery manager's search scope
D. When running the Audit Log Search

318. How do you assign eDiscovery permissions to case members?
A. By modifying existing in-place eDiscovery searches
B. By adding users to an eDiscovery-related role group
C. By enabling Exchange mailbox audit logging
D. By configuring the Audit Log Search

319. What happens to content when an eDiscovery case is closed in the Security & Compliance Center?
A. The content is deleted immediately.
B. The content is archived for long-term storage.
C. Any holds placed on the content are released.
D. The content is transferred to a SupervisoryReview mailbox.

320. What is the primary function of the Productivity App Discovery tool in the Security & Compliance Center?
A. To create new supervision policies
B. To manage eDiscovery cases
C. To see how Office 365 and other cloud service apps are being used
D. To configure content search parameters

321. What is the first step in creating a DLP policy in Office 365?
A. Select the All Locations In Office 365 option.
B. Determine the type of content to protect.

Practice Questions

C. Configure app permissions.
D. Activate the Mobile Device Management service.

322. Where can you select a policy template for creating a DLP policy in Office 365?
A. In the Exchange Admin Center.
B. In the Security & Compliance Center under Policy.
C. On the Cloud App Security App permissions page.
D. On the Mobile Device Management setup page.

323. What is the default option for protecting data in a DLP policy?
A. With People Inside The Organization.
B. Detect when content is shared with external users.
C. Configuring advanced selection settings.
D. Block the user from sending data.

324. What is the purpose of Policy Tips in a DLP policy?
A. To enforce the policy.
B. To activate the Mobile Device Management service.
C. To notify users when they are accessing data that matches the policy.
D. To create an Apple ID for APNs.

325. What can be done after configuring a DLP policy in test mode without Policy Tips?
A. Begin full enforcement of the policy.
B. Use DLP reports to assess the impact.
C. Enroll devices in MDM.
D. Configure an APN certificate for iOS devices.

326. What action can you take if you are confident about the DLP policy configuration?

Practice Questions

A. Test the policy without Policy Tips.
B. Turn on Policy Tips in test mode.
C. Begin full enforcement of the policies.
D. Configure domains for Mobile Device Management.

327. When creating a DLP policy, what can you do to modify the individual rule settings?
A. Choose the All Locations In Office 365 option.
B. Enable Policy Tips.
C. Configure advanced selection settings.
D. Set up multifactor authentication.

328. How can a DLP policy be rolled out gradually?
A. By setting up an APN certificate for iOS devices.
B. By configuring it in test mode without Policy Tips.
C. By directly enforcing all policy rules.
D. By configuring domains for Mobile Device Management.

329. Which role is required to create mobile device management policies in Office 365?
A. Compliance Officer.
B. Global Administrator.
C. Security Administrator.
D. User with App Permissions.

330. What must be configured for managing Apple iOS devices with Office 365 MDM?
A. Multifactor authentication.
B. APNs Certificate.
C. EnterpriseEnrollment and EnterpriseRegistration DNS records.

Practice Questions

D. A DLP policy template.

331. Where within the Security & Compliance Center can you configure additional security policies or organization exclusions from MDM?
A. Data Governance | Import page
B. Data Loss Prevention | Device Security Policies
C. Manage Organization-Wide Device Access settings
D. Mobile Device Management page

332. What type of devices can Office 365 MDM not disable Bluetooth as a setting?
A. Windows Phone 8.1+
B. iOS 6+
C. Samsung Knox
D. Android 4+

333. What can you block on iOS devices through device security policies?
A. Google backup
B. iCloud backup
C. SD card access
D. Exchange ActiveSync

334. What happens to the Retention Hold setting after PST files are imported to an Office 365 mailbox?
A. It is deleted immediately.
B. It is turned off after a set date.
C. It is turned on for an indefinite duration.
D. It does not change.

Practice Questions

335. Which import method requires purchasing hard drives and sending them to an Office 365 data center?
A. Network upload
B. Drive shipping
C. SAS storage blob import
D. Direct server upload

336. What must you do before clicking the '+ New Import Job' button on the Data Governance | Import page?
A. Grant the Mailbox Import Export Role
B. Configure device security policies
C. Turn off Retention Hold
D. Complete a network upload

337. What is the main purpose of the Data Governance section in the Security & Compliance Center?
A. To configure device security policies
B. To manage mobile device access
C. To handle data over its life cycle
D. To monitor the status of the PST import

338. Which of the following is not a valid parameter in the CSV template for the PST Import mapping file?
A. Workload
B. FilePath
C. IsArchive
D. EncryptionMethod

339. Which Office 365 service should you specify in the Workload parameter when importing PST files to user mailboxes?
A. SharePoint

Practice Questions

B. Microsoft Teams
C. Exchange
D. OneDrive for Business

340. What is the role of the AzCopy tool in the PST import process?
A. It generates a SAS URL.
B. It installs the mapping file.
C. It copies PST files to Microsoft Azure.
D. It validates the CSV mapping file.

341. What is the purpose of the RetentionHoldEnabled parameter after completing an import job?
A. To initiate the import job
B. To delete the imported data
C. To enable the processing of retention policies on the mailbox
D. To encrypt the imported data

342. Which type of hard drives are required for drive shipping in a PST import job?
A. External USB hard drives
B. Internal SATA or SAS hard drives
C. Solid-state drives (SSD)
D. Any portable hard drive

343. What should you do if you receive an error stating that not all fields are populated during a drive shipping import job setup?
A. Upload the PST files again
B. Click the Copy The Drive Shipping Key link
C. Restart the computer

Practice Questions

D. Disable the RetentionHoldEnabled parameter

344. Which command is used to encrypt and copy PST files to a hard drive for a drive shipping import job?
A. WAImportExport.exe
B. Set-Mailbox
C. Copy-PSTFiles
D. Encrypt-PST

345. What should you download to prepare the PST Import mapping file?
A. PST Import Tool
B. Azure Import/Export tool
C. PST import mapping file template
D. Office 365 Exchange Online PowerShell endpoint

346. What is the result of enabling an archive mailbox for a user with Exchange Online Plan 2?
A. Users can import PST files directly
B. Users receive unlimited storage space
C. Content older than 2 years is automatically moved to the archive mailbox
D. The RetentionHoldEnabled parameter is set to true

347. What is the purpose of retention policies in Office 365?
A. To encrypt emails
B. To manage the accumulation, retention, and deletion of content
C. To increase storage space
D. To export data to PST files

348. What feature ensures that a retention policy cannot be disabled or made less restrictive?

Practice Questions

A. RetentionHoldEnabled
B. Preservation Lock
C. Drive Shipping Key
D. PST Import mapping

349. How can archive mailboxes be enabled for all users?
A. By selecting each user individually
B. From the Security & Compliance dashboard, by selecting Online Archive Mailbox and Manage
C. Only through the Azure Import/Export tool
D. By using the RetentionHoldEnabled parameter

350. When you select the 'No' button in the drive shipping import process, what is the next step?
A. The filtering criteria page opens
B. The data is immediately imported
C. The final confirmation page opens
D. The import job is canceled

351. Which role must a user have to view service health features in Office 365?
A. User Management Administrator
B. Service Health Administrator
C. Global Administrator
D. Billing Administrator

352. If a user needs to be assigned a role that includes service health, what must you do first?
A. Navigate to the Service Health dashboard
B. Sign in to the Office 365 portal with a Global Administrator account
C. Assign the user as a Customized Administrator
D. Update the user's permissions in the Message Center

Practice Questions

353. Where can you change a user's administrator role in Office 365?
A. In the Service Health dashboard
B. In the Message Center
C. In the Office 365 portal, under Users
D. On the status.office365.com page

354. What should you select to assign the least-privileged administrative role for service health?
A. Global Administrator button
B. Service Administrator checkbox
C. User Management Administrator option
D. Customized Administrator button

355. What are the two views available in the Service Health dashboard?
A. General Availability view and Customized view
B. v1 view and v2 view
C. Basic view and Advanced view
D. Classic view and Modern view

356. What does the 'All Services' tab in the Service Health dashboard display?
A. The status of all messages in the Message Center
B. The status of all user accounts in the tenant
C. The status of all services currently available in the tenant
D. The schedule for planned maintenance events

357. What are the two categories of service incidents?
A. Planned Maintenance and Service Enhancements
B. Unplanned Downtime and Advisories

Practice Questions

C. Planned Maintenance and Unplanned Downtime
D. Service Degradations and Performance Issues

358. What are Advisories in the context of the Service Health dashboard?
A. Announcements for upcoming new features
B. Notifications about user account issues
C. Service degradations resulting in a lower-performing service
D. Summaries of all service incidents

359. Where can you find summaries of notifications for Office 365 services?
A. In the Service Health dashboard
B. In the Active Users page
C. In the Message Center
D. On the status.office365.com page

360. What type of notifications are categorized as 'Plan for Change' in the Message Center?
A. Announcements of past changes
B. Advisories about service health
C. Announcements of future deployment or management changes
D. Summaries of Unplanned Downtime incidents

361. What does Exchange Online use to store its configuration information?
A. Local Active Directory
B. SQL Database
C. Microsoft Entra ID
D. NoSQL Database

362. What are the names of the connectors used in Exchange Online for managing mail flow?
A. Send Connectors and Receive Connectors

Practice Questions

B. Outbound Connectors and Inbound Connectors
C. External Connectors and Internal Connectors
D. SMTP Connectors and POP3 Connectors

363. Which of the following is NOT a recipient type in Exchange Online?
A. Mailboxes
B. Contacts
C. Distribution Groups
D. Nodes

364. What is the maximum number of mailboxes recommended for a cutover migration?
A. 150
B. 500
C. 2000
D. 5000

365. Which migration method requires the use of Microsoft Entra ID Connect (Entra ID Connect)?
A. Cutover migration
B. Staged migration
C. Express migration
D. Hybrid migration

366. What is Autodiscover in the context of Exchange Online?
A. A tool to automatically configure email servers
B. A process used by Microsoft Outlook to determine the mailbox location
C. A feature to discover new updates for Office 365
D. A method to auto-detect spam emails

Practice Questions

367. During the Autodiscover process, what does Outlook query first?
A. HTTPS Root Domain Query
B. Service Connection Point
C. HTTP Redirect Method
D. SRV Record Query

368. Which migration method is also known as minimal hybrid migration?
A. Cutover migration
B. Staged migration
C. Express migration
D. Hybrid migration

369. For which of the following environments can you use a hybrid migration?
A. Exchange 2003 only
B. Exchange 2010, 2013, or 2016
C. Exchange 2007 with an Exchange 2010 or 2013 server
D. Both B and C

370. In a hybrid configuration, where should you configure Autodiscover DNS records to point to initially?
A. Directly to Office 365
B. To the on-premises mail system
C. To an external DNS hosting service
D. To Microsoft Entra ID

371. What is the purpose of the script available at the provided Technet link?
A. To configure SSL offloading
B. To migrate mailboxes to Office 365
C. To identify duplicate proxy addresses during Entra ID Connect

Practice Questions

synchronization
D. To add domains to the Office 365 tenant

372. What is SSL offloading commonly used for?
A. Terminating SSL connections using network devices
B. Migrating mailboxes to and from Office 365
C. Managing certificates across many servers
D. Both A and C

373. Is SSL offloading supported for Mailbox Replication Service (MRS) traffic?
A. Yes, for all traffic
B. No, MRS expects end-to-end SSL encryption
C. Yes, but only for Outlook Web App traffic
D. Yes, but only with a separate virtual IP interface

374. Why is it important to update servers with Windows and Exchange updates before migration?
A. To ensure compatibility with Office 365
B. To decommission Exchange from the on-premises environment
C. Updates can include essential performance, security, or feature enhancements
D. To manage Active Directory objects on-premises

375. What is the result of synchronizing on-premises mailboxes to Office 365?
A. They become mail-enabled users in Exchange Online
B. They are converted to contacts in Office 365
C. They are managed only on-premises
D. They are automatically migrated to Office 365

Practice Questions

376. How is the relationship between on-premises objectGuid and the cloud ImmutableID expressed?
A. [system.convert]:: ToBase64String(objectGuid).ToByteArray()
B. [system.convert]:: ToString(objectGuid)
C. [system.convert]::ToGuid(ImmutableID)
D. [system. convert]:: FromBase64String(ImmutableID)

377. Which cmdlet can you run to check the details of an Exchange certificate used for hybrid configuration?
A. Check-ExchangeCertificate
B. Get-ExchangeCertificate
C. Test-ExchangeCertificate
D. Verify-ExchangeCertificate

378. What should be done if a mailbox has proxy addresses for domains not confirmed in the Office 365 tenant?
A. Leave the addresses as they are
B. Update the DNS records
C. Remove the addresses from the mailbox prior to migration
D. Add the unconfirmed domains to the Office 365 tenant

379. For successful Autodiscover and cross-premises mail routing, what do mailboxes need to have?
A. A verified domain in the tenant
B. An SSL certificate
C. A target proxy address matching .mail.onmicrosoft.com
D. An on-premises user account

380. What is the function of the Hybrid Configuration Wizard in the context of email address templates?
A. It confirms domain ownership through DNS record registration
B. It removes all domains from mailboxes
C. It adds the tenant mail routing domain to all the email address

Practice Questions

templates
D. It migrates mailboxes to Office 365

381. What is the primary role of Microsoft Entra ID in Office 365?
A. To provide email services
B. To act as the foundational service for online services
C. To host websites and web applications
D. To manage Windows updates

382. Which module do you need to install to manage Skype for Business Online via PowerShell?
A. AzureADPreview
B. MSOnline
C. Microsoft Online Services Module
D. Skype for Business Online Connector

383. What is the purpose of the Get-MsolUser cmdlet in Microsoft Entra ID?
A. To create a new user
B. To retrieve user objects
C. To delete a user
D. To modify user properties

384. Which module allows management of Microsoft Entra ID via PowerShell?
A. AzureADPreview
B. MSOnline
C. Both A and B
D. Skype for Business Online Connector

Practice Questions

385. What is required when assigning a license to a user in Microsoft Entra ID?
A. A user's phone number
B. The user's location
C. A user's manager
D. The user's group membership

386. Which PowerShell cmdlet is used to create a new user in Microsoft Entra ID?
A. Get-MsolUser
B. Set-MsolUser
C. New-MsolUser
D. Remove-MsolUser

387. How can you manage an Office 365 user's email properties?
A. Through the Microsoft Entra ID admin center
B. Using the Exchange Online PowerShell module
C. By modifying the user's properties in SharePoint Online
D. Via the Skype for Business Online admin center

388. What is the result of the Remove-MsolUser cmdlet?
A. It updates user properties.
B. It retrieves user objects.
C. It creates a new user.
D. It removes a user object from the Microsoft Entra ID.

389. Which component must be installed to use the older Microsoft Entra ID cmdlets?
A. .NET Framework 4.5 or later
B. Windows PowerShell 5.1
C. Entra ID Preview Module
D. Skype for Business Online Connector

Practice Questions

390. What is the purpose of the Connect-MsolService cmdlet?
A. To disconnect from an Entra ID session
B. To manage SharePoint Online
C. To connect to the Microsoft Entra ID service
D. To install the required PowerShell modules

391. Which PowerShell cmdlet is used to remove a user from Microsoft Entra ID and also from the recycle bin?
A. Get-MsolUser
B. Add-MsolRoleMember
C. Remove-MsolUser
D. New-MsolGroup

392. How can you create a contact in the Office 365 Admin Center?
A. Use the New-MsolUser cmdlet
B. Use the Add-MsolRoleMember cmdlet
C. Navigate to Users > Contacts and add a contact
D. Use the Get-MsolRole cmdlet

393. What is the purpose of the Get-MsolRole cmdlet?
A. To create a new role in Entra ID
B. To remove a role from Entra ID
C. To list all roles in Entra ID
D. To modify an existing role in Entra ID

394. Which of the following is NOT a type of group in Entra ID and Office 365?
A. Microsoft Online roles
B. Distribution groups

Practice Questions

C. Modern groups
D. Resource mailboxes

395. How can you add a user to a specific role in Entra ID using PowerShell?
A. Add-MsolUser
B. Set-MsolUser
C. Add-MsolRoleMember
D. New-MsolGroup

396. What is a mail-enabled user in Exchange Online?
A. A user with a security principal and a mailbox
B. A user with a mailbox who can send emails only
C. A contact overlaid with an Microsoft Entra ID security principal
D. A distribution list with an assigned mailbox

397. Which cmdlet should you use to create a security group in Entra ID through PowerShell?
A. Get-MsolGroup
B. New-MsolGroup
C. Add-MsolGroupMember
D. Set-MsolGroup

398. When creating a group in the Office 365 Admin Center, which of the following options allows the group to receive messages from Internet users?
A. Enabling the RequireSenderAuthenticationEnabled parameter to $true
B. Disabling the RequireSenderAuthenticationEnabled parameter to $false
C. Enabling the IsPublic parameter to $true
D. Setting the ManagedBy parameter

Practice Questions

399. What type of mailbox is used for anything that a user can check out or reserve?
A. Regular mailbox
B. Room mailbox
C. Equipment mailbox
D. Shared mailbox

400. How do unified groups appear when using the Get-MsolGroup cmdlet?
A. As security groups
B. As distribution lists
C. As mail-enabled users
D. They do not appear in the Get-MsolGroup cmdlet

401. Which migration option is recommended for a customer using Exchange Server 2003 and Exchange Server 2007 without deploying a newer version of Exchange?
A. Cutover Migration
B. Staged Migration
C. Full Hybrid Migration
D. Express Migration

402. Where can you select the migration type in the Exchange Admin Center?
A. Dashboard
B. Recipients | Migration
C. Settings | Services
D. Users | Active Users

403. What is the recommended migration option for Exchange 2010, Exchange 2013, and Exchange 2016?

Practice Questions

A. Cutover Migration
B. Staged Migration
C. Full Hybrid Migration
D. Not available

404. What does "Available, not recommended" imply for a migration option?
A. The migration will not work at all.
B. The migration toolset is not compatible.
C. The migration will work but may result in a poor user experience.
D. The migration is the optimal choice.

405. When using multifactor authentication, which module should be installed to connect to Exchange Online with Windows PowerShell?
A. Microsoft Exchange Online Basic Authentication Module
B. Microsoft Exchange Online PowerShell Module
C. Microsoft Entra ID Authentication Library
D. Windows PowerShell Credential Module

406. What is the default setting for MaxConcurrentMigrations in the Office 365 Admin portal or the Exchange Admin Center?
A. 10
B. 20
C. 150
D. 300

407. Which parameter must be less than or equal to the MaxConcurrentMigrations parameter?
A. MaxConcurrentIncrementalSyncs
B. MaxSimultaneousConnections

Practice Questions

C. MaxMigrationVelocity
D. MaxEndpointConnections

408. How many total MaxConcurrentMigrations connections are available per tenant?
A. 20
B. 100
C. 300
D. 600

409. What is the designed user limit for a cutover migration process?
A. 1000 users
B. 1500 users
C. 2000 users
D. 2500 users

410. What blocks the cutover migration option in the Exchange Admin Center?
A. Having more than 2000 users
B. Using Exchange Server 2010 or newer
C. Deploying Entra ID Connect and synchronizing the directory at least once
D. Using multifactor authentication

411. What issue did the migration encounter?
A. Incorrect MX record configuration
B. Mailboxes exceeded the storage limit
C. Administrator did not have proper permission to source mailboxes
D. Autodiscover endpoint was improperly configured

Practice Questions

412. How many objects were finalized in the migration process described?
A. 13
B. 15
C. 2000
D. Not specified

413. After fixing mailbox permissions, what is the first post-migration step for a cutover migration?
A. Assign Office 365 licenses to the migrated users
B. Change the MX Record to refer to Exchange Online
C. Re-create user profiles for Outlook
D. Remove the internal service connection point in the Exchange

414. When should the internal Service Connection Point (SCP) in Exchange be removed?
A. Before starting the migration batch
B. Immediately after the MX Record change
C. After assigning Office 365 licenses
D. For Exchange Server 2007 and later, after the migration

415. Which Exchange versions are eligible for a staged migration process?
A. Exchange Server 2003 and 2007 only
B. Exchange Server 2010 and later
C. All versions of Exchange
D. Exchange Server 2003 and 2010 only

416. What is the minimum required Office 365 license for the migrated users?
A. Business Premium
B. Enterprise E3
C. Exchange Online
D. Any Office 365 license

417. What must be disabled on source mailboxes before performing a staged Exchange migration?
A. Unified Messaging
B. Autodiscover
C. Directory Synchronization
D. Outlook Anywhere

418. What is the purpose of the migration.csv file in a staged Exchange migration?
A. To configure the new Exchange Online environment
B. To create a backup of the user mailboxes
C. To specify which user mailboxes will be migrated
D. To store the new passwords for Office 365 users

419. What happens if you set a password for a federated account in the migration.csv file?
A. The account will be locked
B. The migration will proceed without issues
C. An error will occur
D. The password will be reset upon the next login

420. What migration option becomes unavailable due to enabling Entra ID Connect and Directory Synchronization in the tenant?
A. Staged Migration
B. Cutover Migration
C. Hybrid Migration
D. Express Migration

Practice Questions

421. What is the primary structural and administrative unit in the Yammer organization?
A. Group
B. User
C. Network
D. External network

422. Who can join an internal network on Yammer?
A. Any user with a verified corporate address
B. Any user without a verified corporate address
C. External partners and customers only
D. Anyone with a Yammer account

423. Which of the following is NOT a type of admin role in Yammer?
A. Group admin
B. Network admin
C. Verified admin
D. Global admin

424. Which admin role can configure network settings, features, and applications in Yammer?
A. Group admin
B. Network admin
C. Verified admin
D. All of the above

425. What can group admins NOT do in Yammer?
A. Delete any message
B. Manage user account activity
C. Upload an image for a group
D. Configure network settings

Practice Questions

426. What is the URL to directly access the Yammer administration site?
A. https://portal.office.com/admin
B. https://www.yammer.com
C. https://yammer.com/admin/success
D. https://admin.yammer.com

427. Where can you assign additional network or verified administrators in Yammer?
A. Design screen
B. Users screen
C. Admins screen
D. Analytics screen

428. How can users be invited to join an organization's Yammer network?
A. Through the Bounced Emails screen
B. Through the Block Users screen
C. Through the Invite Users screen
D. Through the Export Users screen

429. What is the purpose of the Network Migration screen in Yammer?
A. To remove users from the network
B. To add stand-alone Yammer networks to the Office 365 tenant
C. To export user data
D. To configure security settings

430. Which admin role can read messages in any private group on Yammer?
A. Group admin
B. Network admin
C. Verified admin
D. All admin roles

Practice Questions

431. What is the maximum file size limit for attachments in Yammer messages?
A. 1 GB
B. 2 GB
C. 5 GB
D. 10 GB

432. Which of the following image formats is NOT supported for the Yammer network logo?
A. GIF
B. JPEG
C. BMP
D. PNG

433. How can a user be granted Network Admin privileges in Yammer?
A. By being granted Global Admin rights in the Office 365 Portal
B. By appointment within the Yammer Admin Center
C. By request to Yammer Support
D. By being the most active user in the network

434. What happens when the Org Chart check box is cleared in Yammer settings?
A. The Org chart is highlighted
B. The Org chart is displayed in a new format
C. The Org chart is disabled and not displayed
D. The Org chart is printed for all users

435. What is the recommended size for the Yammer masthead image?
A. 40 x 160 pixels

Practice Questions

B. 56 x 1200 pixels
C. 50 x 160 pixels
D. 100 x 300 pixels

436. Which setting would you configure to force users to accept the Yammer usage policy upon signup and after any changes?
A. Require users to accept the policy during sign-up and after any changes are made to the policy
B. Display Policy Reminder In the Sidebar
C. Enable Third-Party Applications
D. Clear File Attachment Setting

437. Who can delete files in any public group on Yammer?
A. Any user
B. Network admins
C. Group members
D. Verified admins

438. What must be done to restrict the creation of external networks to only admins in Yammer?
A. Enable Third-Party Applications
B. Select the Only Admins button under External Networks
C. Disable the File Attachment setting
D. Remove all external members from the network

439. What is the recommended size for the Yammer email logo?
A. 40 x 160 pixels
B. 56 x 1200 pixels
C. 50 x 160 pixels
D. 100 x 300 pixels

Practice Questions

440. What is the first step to deleting an external network in Yammer?
A. Select the gear icon and then select Network Admin
B. Scroll to the end of the page and click Delete External Network
C. Select the gear icon and then select your external network
D. Click on the confirmation page

441. What type of network must the parent network be for a Yammer network migration?
A. Stand-alone activated
B. Enterprise activated
C. Office 365 tenant
D. Subsidiary network

442. What happens to the groups and content from the subsidiary network during a Yammer network migration?
A. They are automatically migrated.
B. They are archived but not migrated.
C. They are deleted without backup.
D. They are not migrated and must be exported to be preserved.

443. Can Yammer networks that are part of Office 365 tenants be migrated or consolidated?
A. Yes, without limitations.
B. Only with special permissions.
C. No, they cannot be migrated or consolidated.
D. Yes, but only the users will be migrated

444. After a Yammer network migration, what happens to the content from the subsidiary's external networks?
A. It is deleted.
B. It remains available.

Practice Questions

C. It is archived.
D. It is merged with the parent network's content.

445. Who can perform a Yammer network migration?
A. Any user with administrative privileges.
B. Only Office 365 global admins.
C. The subsidiary network admin.
D. Any user with a verified email.

446. What is the fate of a user that exists in both the parent and subsidiary network post-migration?
A. The user is duplicated in the parent network.
B. The user's subsidiary account is promoted to the parent network.
C. The account in the subsidiary network is deleted.
D. Both accounts remain active.

447. Can data be imported into a Yammer network after it has been exported during a migration?
A. Yes, through the user interface.
B. Yes, using the Yammer API.
C. No, data cannot be imported back into a Yammer network.
D. Yes, but only manually.

448. What is a prerequisite for starting a network migration in Yammer?
A. The subsidiary network must be a stand-alone network.
B. The subsidiary email domain must be part of your tenant.
C. The parent network must have a larger user base.
D. All users must consent to the migration.

449. What should you do before starting a Yammer network migration regarding users?
A. Promote all users to admins.

Practice Questions

B. Ensure all users are active.
C. Notify users about the migration and recommend backups.
D. Delete inactive users.

450. Can a network migration in Yammer be reversed?
A. Yes, within 30 days.
B. Yes, but only by contacting support.
C. No, there is no undo button for network migrations.
D. Yes, if no data has been altered post-migration.

451. What is required to access OneDrive for Business Online?
A. A web browser only
B. A license that includes SharePoint Online or OneDrive for Business
C. A Microsoft account
D. A Windows operating system

452. Where can you find the OneDrive for Business Online access point?
A. https://onedrive.live.com
B. https://portal.office.com
C. https://www.microsoft.com
D. https://sharepoint.com

453. What happens the first time you click the OneDrive tile in the Office 365 dashboard?
A. You are directed to the file upload page.
B. Your OneDrive for Business site is provisioned.
C. The OneDrive sync client starts downloading.
D. You are logged out of the portal.

454. What should you do when the "Welcome to OneDrive" wizard opens?
A. Immediately start uploading documents.

Practice Questions

B. Follow the wizard setup.
C. Click "Not Now" to cancel it.
D. Close the browser.

455. How can you identify which OneDrive sync client you are using in Windows?
A. By checking the version number in the application settings
B. By looking at the color and text of the icon in the system tray
C. By the size of the OneDrive folder on your computer
D. By the speed of file synchronization

456. Where can you initiate the setup for the OneDrive sync client?
A. From the Windows Control Panel
B. From the Office 365 portal or your computer
C. From the Microsoft Store
D. From the Windows Start menu, only

457. What is the file name of the new OneDrive for Business sync client?
A. OneDrive.exe
B. Groove.exe
C. SkyDrive.exe
D. OneDriveSync.exe

458. What is the purpose of the "Sync Your OneDrive Files To This PC" page in the OneDrive setup?
A. To choose the files and folders you want to sync to your PC
B. To update your OneDrive with new files from your PC
C. To select the PC you want to sync files to
D. To set up a backup plan for your PC files

Practice Questions

459. How can you share documents and folders from OneDrive for Business?
A. By moving them to the "Shared" folder
B. By emailing them as attachments
C. By selecting the files or folders and clicking the "Get Link" or "Share" buttons
D. By copying them to a USB drive

460. What happens when you use the "Get Link" option for sharing in OneDrive for Business?
A. A new email message with the link is created.
B. The selected item is moved to a public folder.
C. A link is created which grants edit permission to the recipient.
D. The file is automatically downloaded for the recipient.

461. Where do you need to navigate in the SharePoint Admin Center to set up a My Site Secondary Admin?
A. User Profiles
B. Site Collections
C. Apps
D. Settings

462. What PowerShell command is used to retrieve a list of domain GUIDs for restricting PC synchronization?
A. Get-SPSite
B. Get-ADDomain
C. Get-ADForest
D. Get-DomainGuidList

463. How can you restrict SharePoint and OneDrive for Business access based on network location?
A. By enabling firewall rules

Practice Questions

B. By configuring device access settings
C. By controlling access based on network location
D. By setting up a VPN

464. Which option do you enable to restrict the sharing of OneDrive content with external users?
A. Let Users Share OneDrive Content With External Users
B. Limit External Sharing By Domain
C. Control Access From Apps
D. Mobile Application Management

465. What should you do to apply My Site Secondary Admin privileges to existing sites?
A. Add users individually to each site
B. Use a script and process from the provided link
C. Repeat the setup process
D. Contact Microsoft support

466. Which of the following is NOT a valid file restriction in OneDrive for Business synchronization?
A. Files larger than 2 GB
B. Files with a path longer than 400 characters
C. Files named with a leading period
D. Files named with a leading underscore

467. How can you disable OneDrive provisioning for everyone except certain individuals or groups?
A. By selecting 'Everyone Except External Users' and enabling 'Create Personal Site.'
B. By selecting 'Everyone Except External Users' and disabling 'Create Personal Site.'

Practice Questions

C. By removing all users from the SharePoint license
D. By contacting Office 365 support

468. What happens if you remove a user's SharePoint license?
A. They gain access to OneDrive for Business
B. Their OneDrive site is provisioned immediately
C. They lose access to OneDrive for Business and might lose data
D. Their OneDrive site's sharing settings are reset

469. Which setting can you configure to restrict access on devices that don't support conditional access policies?
A. Mobile Application Management
B. Control Access Based On Network Location
C. Control Access From Apps That Can't Enforce Device-Based Restrictions
D. Allow Syncing Only On PCs Joined To Specific Domains

470. What is the maximum file size that can be synchronized through the OneDrive sync client?
A. 10 GB
B. 15 GB
C. 2 GB
D. 5 GB

471. To configure the Managed Metadata service in SharePoint, where must you first navigate in the SharePoint Central Administration?
A. Application Management
B. System Settings
C. Manage Web Applications
D. Service Applications

Practice Questions

472. What should you do if the Managed Metadata web service is not listed under Service Applications?
A. Start the Managed Metadata web service
B. Navigate to System Settings
C. Click New and select Managed Metadata Services
D. Restart SharePoint Central Administration

473. When creating a new My Site Host site collection, under which tab do you select the My Site Host template?
A. Web Applications
B. System Settings
C. Template Selection
D. Site Collections

474. What is the correct sequence for starting the User Profile service in SharePoint Central Administration?
A. Manage Web Applications > Start Profile Synchronization
B. System Settings > Manage Services On Server > Start User Profile Service
C. Service Applications > New > User Profile Service Application
D. Manage Services On Server > Application Management > Start User Profile Service

475. What are the consequences of starting the User Profile Synchronization Service before configuring the rest of the User Profile service?
A. It will enhance the performance of the configuration steps.
B. It will cause the rest of the configuration steps to fail.
C. It will delete all existing user profiles.
D. It will automatically configure the service.

476. Which service stores information about SharePoint app licenses and permissions?

Practice Questions

A. User Profile service
B. Managed Metadata service
C. App Management service
D. SharePoint Foundation Subscription Settings service

477. Where is the SharePoint Foundation Subscription Settings service configured?
A. SharePoint Central Administration
B. Internet Information Services (IIS)
C. SharePoint Management Shell
D. Office 365 admin center

478. What is required for SharePoint Server to consume resources and content from SharePoint Online or Office 365?
A. Server-to-server authentication
B. User Profile Synchronization Service
C. App Management Service
D. Managed Metadata web service

479. What kind of synchronization should you start after configuring a new connection for user profiles?
A. Full Profile Synchronization
B. Incremental Profile Synchronization
C. Active Directory Synchronization
D. App Management Synchronization

480. To enable Hybrid OneDrive for Business, which SharePoint Online permissions must users have?
A. Manage Web Applications and Manage Services On Server
B. Create a Personal Site, and Follow People, and Edit your Profile
C. Configure Synchronization Connections and Manage User Permissions
D. Start Profile Synchronization and Manage Service Applications

Practice Questions

481. What is the default setting for storage management in SharePoint Online?
A. Manual Storage Operation
B. Automatic Storage Operation
C. No Storage Operation
D. Custom Storage Operation

482. Which user interface is enabled by default in OneDrive for Business?
A. No User Interface
B. Classic Experience
C. New Experience
D. Hybrid Experience

483. What is the default setting for the Sync Client for SharePoint when a user clicks the Sync button in a SharePoint library?
A. Start The New Client
B. No Sync Client
C. Start The Old Client
D. Disable The Sync Client

484. What is SharePoint Online's default setting for the Admin Center Experience?
A. Use Basic
B. Use Advanced
C. No Admin Center
D. Custom Admin Center

485. By default, what is the setting for the Enterprise Social Collaboration platform in SharePoint Online?
A. Use SharePoint Newsfeed

Practice Questions

B. Use Yammer
C. Use Both
D. Use Neither

486. What does the default setting for Site Pages in SharePoint Online allow users to do?
A. Prevent Users From Creating Site Pages
B. Review Users' Site Pages
C. Allow Users To Create Site Pages
D. Delete Users' Site Pages

487. In the context of SharePoint Online, what does IRM stand for?
A. Internal Rights Management
B. Information Rights Management
C. Integrated Resource Management
D. Intellectual Rights Management

488. What is the default setting for Mobile Push Notifications – OneDrive for Business?
A. Disable Notifications
B. Enable Notifications
C. Enable Notifications for Selected Users
D. No Notifications Available

489. What is the default behavior for the Comments on Site Pages setting in SharePoint Online?
A. Disable Comments On-Site Pages
B. Enable Comments On-Site Pages
C. Enable Moderated Comments On-Site Pages
D. Comments On Site Pages Not Available

Practice Questions

490. Which setting determines whether a SharePoint Online user can create a site with an Office 365 Group or a Classic Site by default?
A. A Site With An Office 365 Group
B. A Classic Site
C. A Site With An Office 365 Group Or A Classic Site
D. No Site Creation Allowed

491. How can Yammer administrators track user activity?
A. Through the Member Directory
B. Through the Account Activity admin screen
C. Via direct email notifications
D. Through regular expression monitoring

492. What should you do to log off an active user session on Yammer?
A. Email the user to log off
B. Click the Logout link next to their name on the Account Activity page
C. Delete the user's account
D. Update the user's profile

493. What is the consequence of blocking a user's email address on Yammer?
A. The user's account is immediately deleted
B. The user cannot join the network
C. All the user's previous posts are removed
D. The user's password is reset

494. What happens to bounced email addresses in Yammer?
A. They are automatically deleted after 30 days
B. They are immediately deactivated

Practice Questions

C. They are listed and can be deactivated by an admin
D. The system ignores them

495. What must be included in the header of a CSV file for Bulk Update in Yammer?
A. User ID, Full Name, Location
B. Action, Email Address, Full Name, Job Title, Password, New Email
C. Email Address, New Email, Password
D. Full Name, Job Title, Department

496. Which value in the action column of a Bulk Update CSV for Yammer will deactivate a user account?
A. New
B. Update
C. Suspend
D. Delete

497. How can administrators customize the profile fields in Yammer?
A. By editing the user's profile directly
B. By selecting or clearing checkboxes in the Profile Fields dialog box
C. It's not possible to customize profile fields
D. By sending a request to Yammer support

498. What is the primary purpose of the Monitor Keywords feature in Yammer?
A. To filter out spam messages
B. To generate notifications of posts matching certain patterns
C. To monitor the user login activity
D. To keep track of popular topics

Practice Questions

499. What happens when a user tries to sign up for Yammer with a blocked email address?
A. They receive a warning message
B. They are redirected to a help page
C. They cannot complete the process and the Sign Up Free button changes to Retry
D. Their account is created but flagged for review

500. What can be exported from the Export Users dialog box in Yammer?
A. Only the user's name and email address
B. A CSV of users including fields like User ID, Email Address, Name, Job Title, Location, and Joined On
C. All user messages and attachments
D. The complete user profile information

Answers

1. Answer: B

Explanation: Immediately after supplying your name, phone number, and email address. The tenant name selection occurs on the User ID creation page right after you've chosen your preferred Office 365 subscription and provided your details.

2. Answer: C

Explanation: All Office 365 and Microsoft Azure tenants end with the onmicrosoft.com name; this suffix is a permanent part of the tenant's URL and user log-ons.

3. Answer: C

Explanation: You won't be able to proceed until a unique name is chosen. The process informs you if the "Your Company" portion of the sign-in ID is in use and requires a unique name to proceed.

4. Answer: C

Explanation: No, it cannot be changed. Once you have selected a tenant name and clicked the "Create My Account" button, your tenant name is permanently set.

5. Answer: B

Explanation: In Exchange Online, the tenant name is included in the routing email address for every mail-enabled object you create. This address,

Answers

formatted as `<username>@<tenantname>.onmicrosoft.com`, is used for internal routing, service identification, and as a fallback address.

6. Answer: C

Explanation: In SharePoint Online, the tenant name appears in the URLs for internal navigation and external sharing requests. This inclusion helps in identifying the specific tenant associated with the SharePoint site and its resources.

7. Answer: B

Explanation: It's an optional service routing address. Referred to as the service routing address, it is added to mail-enabled objects during the Exchange hybrid setup if chosen.

8. Answer: B

Explanation: The tenant name's relevance after merger, acquisition, or divestiture. It's important to ensure that the tenant name would still be applicable if the company undergoes any significant changes.

9. Answer: C

Explanation: In the sharing URLs and browser address bar. In OneDrive, the tenant name is included in the URL when sharing files and is visible in the address bar while navigating between folders or files. This helps identify the specific tenant associated with the OneDrive account.

10. Answer: B

Answers

Explanation: As a mandatory routing address that cannot be changed. Exchange Online automatically assigns this email address to every mail-enabled object.

11. **Answer: D**

Explanation: The tenant name in Skype for Business is visible in the meeting URL found in meeting requests sent by email. Users can view this by right-clicking or hovering over the 'Join Skype Meeting' hyperlink in the email invites.

12. **Answer: B**

Explanation: The tenant name is not visible when viewing the properties of Office Pro Plus applications or in any additional licensed Office suite applications such as Microsoft Visio or Project.

13. **Answer: C**

Explanation: Office Online applications show the tenant name in the browser address bar as OneDrive for Business is used as the default save location for newly created documents.

14. **Answer: C**

Explanation: After a trial subscription expires, you must either start paying for that subscription or select another plan to continue using the services.

15. **Answer: C**

Explanation: During the trial subscription period, you can set up the tenant, sync users, and assign them licenses to start testing the service.

Answers

16. Answer: C

Explanation: The four basic technologies present in Office 365 are Exchange, Skype, SharePoint, and Office Pro Plus.

17. Answer: A

Explanation: The plans for Office 365 are divided into categories such as Small Business, Education, Government, Nonprofit, and Home Use.

18. Answer: C

Explanation: It is impossible to provide a single answer as to what the best possible Office 365 plan because the plans are constantly evolving, and the license selection process is complex.

19. Answer: C

Explanation: Office Online applications automatically use OneDrive for Business as the default save location for newly created documents.

20. Answer: C

Explanation: After the trial subscription expires, you can choose to renew the licenses that you have already chosen or you can add completely different licenses.

21. Answer: C

Answers

Explanation: Office 365 Business plans are suitable for organizations with fewer than 300 users. If you have more than 300 users or plan to exceed that number in the next one or two years, it's recommended to consider Office 365 Enterprise.

22. Answer: C

Explanation: Office 365 Business plans do not provide unified communications options such as PSTN conferencing or Cloud PBX, which are available in Enterprise plans.

23. Answer: B

Explanation: In Office 365, shared mailboxes that exceed 50 GB in size require a license. This policy is in place to ensure fair resource allocation and to encourage proper management of mailbox sizes within organizations. If you have shared mailboxes that exceed this limit, you would need to assign an appropriate license to them to maintain access and functionality.

24. Answer: B

Explanation: The Office 365 Enterprise E3 license includes Office Pro Plus, Exchange Rights Management, and the eDiscovery Center, along with other features.

25. Answer: B

Explanation: Advanced eDiscovery and Customer Lockbox. The Office 365 Enterprise E5 license offers additional features over the E3 plan, including Advanced eDiscovery, Customer Lockbox, Power BI Pro, and Delve Analytics.

Answers

26. Answer: D

Explanation: The Office 365 Enterprise F1 license is designed for users to access email, calendaring, instant messaging, and other web-based features without requiring a full-featured workstation.

27. Answer: C

Explanation: Office 365 Nonprofit plans are available for organizations that qualify for Nonprofit status and offer the same features as the corresponding Enterprise plans at a discounted price.

28. Answer: D

Explanation: Office 365 Education plans are free to students and teachers, but the organization must qualify to receive the plan.

29. Answer: B

Explanation: Non-delivery errors when replying to old emails often occur because an x500 address, which contains the LegacyExchangeDN value, is missing from the proxy addresses list for the recipient in Exchange Online.

30. Answer: A

Explanation: Office 365 Government plans ensure that all services comply with federal requirements, content is stored in the United States only, and access is restricted to screened Microsoft personnel.

31. Answer: C

Answers

Explanation: The current subscriptions can be viewed in the Office 365 Admin Center by selecting Billing from the Admin menu and then choosing Subscriptions.

32. Answer: D

Explanation: By clicking on a single subscription in the Office 365 portal, you can view detailed statistics about that subscription, including cost per user per year, the total number of licenses owned and in use, and the expiration date for the subscription.

33. Answer: C

Explanation: The Global Administrator role has unrestricted access to all features of the tenant and underlying Microsoft Entra ID. It is equivalent to the Domain Administrator role in on-premises Active Directory.

34. Answer: C

Explanation: The Billing Administrator can view users, groups, and contacts in the tenant but cannot modify or delete them, nor can they assign licenses.

35. Answer: C

Explanation: The User Management Administrator role can create and delete users, groups, and contacts, as well as set user licenses and reset passwords.

36. Answer: C

Answers

Explanation: The Billing Administrator role can manage billing and subscription services, including viewing and modifying subscription and billing details.

37. Answer: B

Explanation: The Services Administrator can access service settings and subscription services, view company information and service health, and manage support tickets but cannot modify subscription or billing details, assign licenses, or reset passwords.

38. Answer: D

Explanation: Hybrid is a common term used when discussing Office 365 deployment options, and it refers to a deployment that combines on-premises infrastructure with cloud services.

39. Answer: B

Explanation: It is important to understand what a hybrid deployment entails before deciding to configure it, as it will influence the necessary infrastructure and setup tasks.

40. Answer: C

Explanation: It's important to ensure that all necessary updates are tested, approved, and applied, including any Office or Outlook updates, to avoid issues such as delegation problems during migration.

41. Answer: C

Answers

Explanation: The Exchange hybrid configuration allows for a seamless integration between on-premises Exchange and Exchange Online. One of the key features includes cross-premises calendaring, which allows users to share calendar information between the two environments.

42. **Answer: A**

Explanation: Directory synchronization between on-premises and Office 365 is a prerequisite for setting up Exchange hybrid mode. It ensures that user identities are consistent across both environments.

43. **Answer. B**

Explanation: The Exchange Mailbox Replication Service is responsible for preserving the Microsoft Outlook profile and Offline Store (OST) file after a mailbox is moved from on-premises to Exchange Online.

44. **Answer: C**

Explanation: The one-way outbound topology for SharePoint hybrid supports search capabilities, allowing the on-premises SharePoint farm to connect outbound to SharePoint Online.

45. **Answer: B**

Explanation: A reverse proxy in the SharePoint hybrid configuration is used to enable users to navigate between SharePoint Online and the on-premises SharePoint farm.

46. **Answer: C**

Answers

Explanation: The two-way hybrid topology for SharePoint supports both search and Business Connectivity Services (BCS), allowing for connectivity and service sharing between on-premises and SharePoint Online.

47. **Answer: C**

Explanation: In a SharePoint hybrid environment, searches are performed in two stages, one for each environment, and the results are displayed in separate result blocks.

48. **Answer: C**

Explanation: The Skype hybrid configuration allows for the migration of user data, such as contact lists and scheduled meetings, between on-premises Skype/Lync servers and Skype for Business Online, ensuring continuity for users.

49. **Answer: C**

Explanation: An internet-facing Exchange 2013 (or later) Client Access Server (CAS) and Mailbox server (MBX) roles are prerequisites for setting up an Exchange hybrid environment.

50. **Answer: B**

Explanation: The Active Directory forest-functional level must be at least Windows Server 2003 or later for an Exchange hybrid configuration to be implemented.

51. **Answer: C**

Answers

Explanation: The first step is to navigate to "https://products.office.com". This is where you can select the Office 365 plan you wish to use and begin the process of setting up your subscription.

52. **Answer: C**

Explanation: The tenant name you select during Office 365 setup is permanent and becomes the brand for your subscription, so choosing wisely is crucial.

53. **Answer: A**

Explanation: After selecting an Office 365 plan, the options available are either Free Trial or Buy Now to start your Office 365 tenant creation, as indicated in the steps for signing up.

54. **Answer: C**

Explanation: In Microsoft Office 365, users assigned the Global Administrator role have the authority to create other Global Administrators. This is a powerful capability designed to allow organizations to delegate administrative responsibilities as needed while maintaining control over user access and security. It's essential to manage Global Administrator privileges carefully to prevent unauthorized access to sensitive data and configurations.

55. **Answer: B**

Explanation: To add a new administrative account with User administration privileges, you should select "Add A User" from the Home page

Answers

56. Answer: A

Explanation: The "Global Administrator" role provides full access to all administrative features in Office 365, making it the appropriate choice for setting up an administrator role

57. Answer: B

Explanation: It is recommended that all network devices be updated to their latest versions to ensure they support Office 365 connectivity, as detailed in the section on configuring DNS, firewalls, and proxy servers.

58. Answer: B

Explanation: Configuring public DNS records is necessary to verify domain names and set up the required records for services like Mail Exchanger (MX), Exchange Autodiscover, Skype for Business, etc.

59. Answer: B

Explanation: Any infrastructure changes required to support Office 365 should be made in advance of starting your Office 365 deployment to avoid issues during the setup process.

60. Answer: A

Explanation: After setting up a new Office 365 tenant, the Office 365 portal opens on the Active Users view, where you can begin creating users, editing organizational information, and assigning licenses

61. Answer: B

Answers

Explanation: The first step is to click the 'Go To Setup' button on the Office 365 Admin Center home page, as indicated in the text under the heading starting the Office 365 Enterprise E3 setup process in the Office 365 Portal

62. **Answer: D**

Explanation: If your DNS is managed internally or by a non-GoDaddy entity, you should select 'Add A Verification Record' to manually add the TXT record to your DNS to verify domain ownership.

63. **Answer: A**

Explanation: Upon verifying the domain ownership with GoDaddy, the setup process automatically creates a TXT record in the domain DNS configuration.

64. **Answer: A**

Explanation: To have Office 365 configure DNS records automatically, you should select 'Add Records For Me' during the setup process.

65. **Answer: C**

Explanation: When manually updating DNS records for Office 365, it is necessary to update the Exchange Autodiscover, SIP, MX, and CNAME records.

66. **Answer: C**

Answers

Explanation: If your domain is already configured with DNS records for another service, you should use the manual configuration options and make only the necessary changes to support your Office 365 setup.

67. **Answer: C**

Explanation: When setting up Office 365 for email functionality, updating MX (Mail Exchange) and SPF (Sender Policy Framework) records is essential. The MX records specify the mail servers responsible for receiving emails on behalf of your domain. In contrast, SPF records help prevent email spoofing and ensure legitimate email delivery by specifying which servers are authorized to send emails to your domain. These updates ensure smooth email operation within the Office 365 environment.

68. **Answer: B**

Explanation: While Office 365 does streamline the setup process, including domain registration, it typically requires some manual steps from the user or administrator. This often involves verifying ownership of the domain and configuring DNS records to point to Office 365 services. However, once these steps are completed, Office 365 can effectively manage email, applications, and other services for the registered domain.

69. **Answer: A**

Explanation: To return to the Office 365 portal home page after completing the setup process, you should click 'Go To The Admin Center.'

70. **Answer: B**

Answers

Explanation: The DNS updates enable Microsoft Outlook and mobile client connectivity to your Office 365 tenant, as well as Skype client connectivity.

71. **Answer: B**

Explanation: ` The Microsoft Entra ID (AAD) Connect tool is used to synchronize user identities from an organization's on-premises Active Directory to Microsoft Entra ID, allowing for a unified identity for users of both on-premises and cloud services.

72. **Answer: B**

Explanation: Event ID 107 indicates that Entra ID has redirected the provisioning endpoint service call to an alternate endpoint, which is part of the directory synchronization process.

73. **Answer: B**

Explanation: Event ID 2002 is associated with the informational message that the Entra ID Connect Windows Service (Entra ID Sync) has stopped successfully.

74. **Answer: C**

Explanation: Warning event ID 6110 indicates that the configuration has changed since the last import or sync run profile, and a full import or sync was not performed. The sync engine will continue to report this warning until the issue is resolved.

75. **Answer: D**

Answers

Explanation: The Set-MsolUserLicense cmdlet is used for assigning licenses and service plans to a user, not for setting a Usage Location. The Set-MsolUser cmdlet is used for setting a user's Usage Location.

76. **Answer: C**

Explanation: Event ID 6941 logs each error that occurs during the export run step and is used to identify specific errors such as DataValidationFailed, InvalidSoftMatch, or AttributeValueMustBeUnique.

77. **Answer: B**

Explanation: Microsoft Entra ID group-based licensing requires either Microsoft Entra ID Basic or Premium licenses, which are paid features, to manage Microsoft Entra ID licenses using groups.

78. **Answer: A**

Explanation: Event ID 116 is an informational logging event that returns directory synchronization settings related to the export threshold, machine name, and other details.

79. **Answer: C**

Explanation: Event ID 601 appears for every source Active Directory forest synchronized as a source for the Password Hash Synchronization feature, indicating the Password Synchronization Manager has started.

80. **Answer: C**

Answers

Explanation: Event ID 904 is related to Scheduler and involves informational events such as Scheduler starting, settings changing, and purging Entra ID Connect Operations Run history. These events should be monitored to provide reporting on the standard operation of the Entra ID Connect engine.

81. **Answer: A**

Explanation: Microsoft Defender for Endpoint is a comprehensive endpoint security platform designed to help organizations prevent, detect, investigate, and respond to advanced threats across their Microsoft 365 environment. It provides threat and vulnerability management, attack surface reduction, endpoint detection and response (EDR), and automated investigation and remediation.

82. **Answer: C**

Explanation: To use the Entra ID Connect health dashboard, an Entra ID Premium license is required from the users.

83. **Answer: B**

Explanation: By default, synchronizations with Microsoft Entra ID (AAD) Connect occur every 30 minutes. This interval ensures that changes made in your on-premises Active Directory are regularly synced with Entra ID, keeping both environments up to date. However, it's worth noting that you can adjust the synchronization frequency based on your organization's needs and requirements.

84. **Answer: C**

Answers

Explanation: The Export feature in the Entra ID Connect health dashboard allows you to export all the export errors from every category into a CSV file.

85. Answer: C

Explanation: In the Notification Settings of the Entra ID Connect health dashboard, you can specify who should receive notifications, including all global administrators in Office 365 and other recipients, via email.

86. Answer: A

Explanation: The Sync Error By Type tab in the Entra ID Connect health dashboard allows you to examine the errors that occurred during the last export to Azure, categorized by type.

87. Answer: B

Explanation: In the dashboard, you can click the sync error count to review details about each type of error, which includes information on the object type and attribute that caused the validation.

88. Answer: B

Explanation: Any changes to the Entra ID Connect server configuration can have a significant impact on both the data synchronized to Entra ID and the length of time that synchronization requires.

89. Answer: C

Explanation: An 'object-too-large' error typically refers to the number of values populated on a multivalued attribute on the object, such as having more than the allowed limit for proxy addresses.

Answers

90. **Answer: B**

Explanation: Configuring the technical contact for your tenant ensures that error emails from the Entra ID Connect synchronization process are sent to the appropriate recipient. Without a configured technical contact, error notifications may not be delivered.

91. **Answer: B**

Explanation: Unlike on-premises Active Directory, which is organized hierarchically with organizational units and domains, Microsoft Entra ID has a flat structure. All users, groups, and contacts exist in a single container without organizational boundaries.

92. **Answer: C**

Explanation: Microsoft Entra ID enforces data uniqueness and will not allow objects to have the same value populated for attributes that should be unique, such as UserPrincipalName and ProxyAddresses. This is to prevent authentication issues and problems with mail flow.

93. **Answer: C**

Explanation: The UserPrincipalName attribute must be unique for every object in Entra ID, as it is used for authentication purposes. If there is a conflict, special action is taken to transform that value, rendering the account unusable until the conflict is resolved.

94. **Answer: C**

Answers

Explanation: In Entra ID, only the User and iNetOrgPerson object types have a UserPrincipalName value. Contacts and groups do not have a UserPrincipalName value, which is crucial for authentication within Entra ID.

95. Answer: C

Explanation: When a UserPrincipalName conflict occurs during synchronization to Entra ID, a transformation process is initiated to make the UserPrincipalName unique. However, this renders the account unusable until the underlying conflict is resolved.

96. Answer: D

Explanation: The ProxyAddress attribute is crucial for mail flow in Entra ID. If there are duplicate proxy addresses between objects, it can lead to problems with mail delivery. Entra ID takes steps to remediate such duplication to ensure proper mail flow.

97. Answer: C

Explanation: Duplicate Attribute Residency is a feature introduced to alleviate problems caused by the duplication of attribute values during synchronization to Entra ID. It operates independently of the synchronization engine version and works to resolve conflicts.

98. Answer: A

Explanation: The Duplicate Attribute Resiliency feature was introduced in September 2016 to help address and remediate issues related to the duplication of attributes during synchronization to Entra ID.

Answers

99. Answer: B

Explanation: The most common types of attribute value conflicts during initial synchronization to Entra ID are UserPrincipalName and ProxyAddresses. These conflicts need to be resolved for proper authentication and mail flow.

100. Answer: C

Explanation: If a new user's UserPrincipalName matches one of the proxy addresses of an object already synchronized to Entra ID, the UserPrincipalName will not be allowed. This results in a broken authentication process for the new user until the issue is resolved.

101. Answer: C

Explanation: When a duplicate UserPrincipalName is synchronized to Entra ID, the system automatically quarantines the duplicate value and modifies the UserPrincipalName of the conflicting account by adding a random four-digit number to the prefix, and changing the suffix to @tenant.onmicrosoft.com to ensure uniqueness.

102. Answer: B

Explanation: When you try to assign an Exchange Online license to a user with a quarantined proxy address due to a conflict, the system will display an error indicating that there is a uniqueness violation, and the license cannot be assigned until the proxy address conflict is resolved.

103. Answer: C

Explanation: In case of a proxy address conflict, the duplicate proxy address value is removed from the object being synchronized and placed in a

Answers

quarantined state. This state is maintained indefinitely until the conflict is resolved manually or the offending address is removed from the object.

104. **Answer: D**

Explanation: The Duplicate Attribute Resiliency feature is designed to handle conflicts by quarantining duplicate attributes like UserPrincipalNames and proxy addresses. It sends a notification email to the tenant administrator but does not log an error in the Entra ID Connect tool.

105. **Answer: B**

Explanation: The technical notification email is usually sent to the person identified during tenant setup, which is typically the individual who created the Office 365 subscription.

106. **Answer: B**

Explanation: The technical notification email can be configured in the Office 365 Admin Center portal by editing the organization profile or by using Windows PowerShell commands such as Set-MsolCompanyContactInformation.

107. **Answer: B**

Explanation: For better management and to ensure that more than one administrator receives the notification emails from the synchronization process, it's recommended that the technical notification email setting be configured to use the email address associated with a distribution list in the on-premises Exchange organization.

Answers

108. **Answers: C**

Explanation: Typically, a UserPrincipalName conflict is resolved by Entra ID by adding a four-digit number to the prefix of the UserPrincipalName to ensure its uniqueness.

109. **Answer: B**

Explanation: To locate objects in an error state in the Office 365 Admin Center portal, you log on to Office 365, select Users on the main admin page, and then choose Users With Errors from the Views drop-down list.

110. **Answer: B**

Explanation: For UserPrincipalName and proxy address conflicts, Office 365 sends only one notification email when the conflict is first detected during the synchronization process, and no additional notifications are sent for the same conflict.

111. **Answer: C**

Explanation: Detailed information about objects with synchronization errors can be located using Windows PowerShell with commands like `Get-MsolDirSyncProvisioningError`. The DirSync Status Summary page and the error resolution email can also provide information, but Windows PowerShell is a direct method to view and sort through objects with provisioning errors.

112. **Answer: C**

Answers

Explanation: Entra ID removes the conflicting value from the second or subsequent object that was synchronized with the duplicate value. It doesn't know which object should be the "winner," so the value might not be removed from the correct object.

113. Answer: B

Explanation: A connector space is a holding location that contains a copy of each object from the source directory, along with all the object's attributes. It is used in subsequent steps of synchronization, where objects can be transformed as they flow through the synchronization engine.

114. Answer: C

Explanation: The purpose of the meta directory in Entra ID Connect is to maintain and synchronize objects across the connected directories. This includes evaluating objects, filtering, joining, and transforming them during synchronization.

115. Answer: B

Explanation: Objects that are filtered out during synchronization are still stored in the Entra ID Connect meta directory. They are not exported to Office 365 but can be used later, if necessary, based on the defined configuration.

116. Answer: C

Explanation: The Duplicate Attribute Resiliency feature in Entra ID aligns with the 'PropertyConflict' error category that can be viewed with PowerShell commands.

Answers

117. Answer: B

Explanation: When dealing with a large number of errors, using Windows PowerShell to export a sorted list by provisioning error type to a CSV file is recommended to generate a detailed report and manage the errors effectively.

118. Answer: B

Explanation: Filtering during directory synchronization is a function that eliminates objects that are not desired to be exported to the Office 365 tenant. It is a critical first step in the transformation process of the data.

119. Answer: B

Explanation: Users are typically the main objects you want to synchronize. In contrast, ForeignSecurityPrincipal objects and TPM devices are examples of objects that you might want to filter out but not synchronize.

120. Answer: C

Explanation: The ultimate goal of the meta-directory is to maintain a connection between each object and its partner, as well as any new objects created as a result, so that ongoing changes in any of the directories can be updated on all the connected objects.

121. Answer: B

Explanation: The Express Installation is intended for a quick setup of Office 365 synchronization with a limited number of configuration options, primarily for single Active Directory forest environments.

Answers

122. Answer: C

Explanation: The on-premises Active Directory account must be a member of the Enterprise Administrators group because it is used to create a service account that will be used for the permanent synchronization process.

123. Answer: A

Explanation: The On-Premises Directory Synchronization Service Account is named:

Sync_SERVERNAME_randomGUID@yourtenant.onmicrosoft.com and is a standard user account.

124. Answer: B

Explanation: The service account is granted Replicating Directory Changes, and Replicating Directory Changes All permissions at the top level of the forest to support password synchronization.

125. Answer: C

Explanation: During Express Installation, the wizard checks if the UserPrincipalName suffixes can be used for authentication with Office 365 and warns if any suffix is non-routable or not added to the Entra ID domain.

126. Answer: C

Explanation: If your environment consists of more than one Active Directory forest or has other specific requirements, you must use the custom installation method.

Answers

127. Answer: B

Explanation: A standard user account, not a Global Administrator account, named Sync_SERVERNAME_randomGUID@yourtenant.onmicrosoft.com, is automatically created in your Entra ID tenant.

128. Answer: B

Explanation: A non-routable UPN suffix would result in an inability for users to log on to Office 365 using their UPN or email address, and federated authentication like Active Directory Federation Service (AD FS) would not be possible.

129. Answer: C

Explanation: Selecting the Exchange Hybrid Deployment checkbox adds additional rules to the configuration that enable writeback of select Exchange-related Active Directory attributes from Microsoft Entra ID to on-premises Active Directory.

130. Answer: A

Explanation: If the 'Start The Synchronization Process When Configuration Completes' checkbox is selected, the Entra ID Connect installation begins synchronizing users to Office 365 immediately after the installation process completes.

131. Answer: C

Explanation: Custom installation allows for specifying a custom installation location for the Entra ID Connect binaries, while Express installation does

Answers

not offer this level of customization and assumes preferred configuration options for a quick setup.

132. Answer: A

Explanation: Microsoft 365 Business Basic is designed for small to medium-sized businesses that need essential productivity tools like Exchange Online, OneDrive, SharePoint, and Microsoft Teams, along with basic security features. This plan offers cost-effective access to cloud services without the advanced security, compliance, and management features found in higher-tier plans like Microsoft 365 Enterprise E5 and Microsoft 365 Business Premium. Office 365 E3 is more suitable for larger enterprises needing advanced features beyond basic requirements.

133. Answer: C
Explanation: A directory named Microsoft Microsoft Entra ID Connect is automatically created in the C:\Program Files directory and should not be deleted after installation.

134. Answer: C

Explanation: Entra ID Connect supports up to 100,000 Active Directory objects when using the included Microsoft SQL Server Express edition.

135. Answer: D

Explanation: If the environment has more than 100,000 objects, you must install Entra ID Connect using a full version of Microsoft SQL Server.

136. Answer: C

Answers

Explanation: The theoretical object limit for Entra ID Connect using SQL Server Express is based on the size of the SQL database, which is restricted to 10 GB.

137. Answer: C

Explanation: The account must have administrative permissions (SQL SA) within SQL, or the Entra ID Connect installation will fail.

138. Answer: B

Explanation: When Entra ID Connect is installed, a local security group called "ADSyncAdmins" is created on the server where Entra ID Connect is installed. Members of this group are granted full rights to manage the Entra ID Connect tool, including configuring synchronization settings, monitoring synchronization status, and managing connectors. This group is essential for delegating administrative tasks related to Entra ID Connect while ensuring proper access control and security.

139. Answer: D

Explanation: The user account used to perform the Entra ID Connect installation is automatically placed in the ADSyncAdmins group when the installation completes.

140. Answer: B

Explanation: If specifying custom sync groups in Custom mode for Entra ID Connect, the groups must be created prior to installation. Failure to do so will cause the installer to fail.

Answers

141. Answer: C

Explanation: To use the Password Writeback feature, the user must be licensed for Entra ID Premium. An Entra ID Premium P1 or P2 license or the Enterprise Mobility Suite (EMS) license is required to enable this feature.

142. Answer: D

Explanation: The password writeback feature in Entra ID Connect supports both federated users using AD FS and synchronized users with Password Sync enabled. It allows users to reset passwords in Entra ID, ensuring changes are synchronized back to on-premises AD.

143. Answer: D

Explanation: The process often begins by logging on to the Office 365 portal and selecting the Admin tile. This grants access to the Office 365 admin center, where administrators can manage various aspects of their Office 365 subscription, such as user accounts, licenses, security settings, and more. From there, administrators can initiate tasks like setting up users, configuring services, managing domains, and accessing various administrative tools and reports.

144. Answer: B

Explanation: Group writeback requires the on-premises Exchange organization to be a minimum of Exchange 2013 CU8 or later.

145. Answer: C

Explanation: The Group Writeback feature is for Office 365 groups only; security and distribution groups are not supported.

Answers

146. Answer: C

Explanation: It is necessary to use the MSOnline Windows PowerShell module to enable device writeback in Active Directory.

147. Answer: B

Explanation: The Directory Extensions attribute sync is limited to a total of 100 additional attributes.

148. Answer: A

Explanation: After selecting Authentication Methods, you must select the box for each method type that you want to allow for password reset.

149. Answer: C

Explanation: Staging mode enables the Entra ID Connect server to operate in a read-only mode, where it reads from the Active Directory and applies synchronization rules but does not export any changes to Entra ID.

150. Answer: C

Explanation: Upon successful entry of the challenge information in the password reset portal, the user can reset their password, and that password change is written back to on-premises Active Directory.

151. Answer: C

Answers

Explanation: After the installation of Entra ID Connect, the Configuration Complete page is provided to summarize the installation's outcome, including the status, any warnings about the environment, and the synchronization status. This allows the installer to review any notifications or warnings and take necessary actions if required.

152. Answer: D

Explanation: The Entra ID Connect Configuration Documenter is recommended for backing up the Entra ID Connect configuration. It can be used to generate an HTML report of your configuration and allows for reporting on differences between configuration backups.

153. Answer: B

Explanation: Precedence in Entra ID Connect synchronization rules is a numerical value that indicates the order of importance of the rules. The lower the numerical value, the higher the precedence and priority the rule has during the synchronization process.

154. Answer: C

Explanation: When creating synchronization rules in Entra ID Connect, precedence determines the order in which rules are applied. Lower numerical precedence values take precedence over higher ones. Therefore, to force a different attribute value than what is set by existing rules, you would create a new rule with a lower numerical precedence value than the existing rule. This ensures that the new rule takes precedence and overrides the attribute value set by the existing rule.

155. Answer: A

Answers

Explanation: When objects from different forests are configured to join on attributes such as Mail, the order in which the forests were added to the Entra ID Connect Wizard affects the resulting objects synchronized to Entra ID. The forest added first will have synchronization rules with higher precedence (lower numeric value).

156. Answer: C

Explanation: To ensure a specific value from a particular forest takes precedence, you should clone the synchronization rule(s) that flow those attributes and assign them higher precedence (a lower numerical value) than the existing rules.

157. Answer: A

Explanation: The command `Start-ADSyncSyncCycle` is used in PowerShell to initiate the synchronization process immediately in Entra ID Connect.

158. Answer: B

Explanation: The Entra ID Connect staging mode is designed to provide a secondary, warm-standby server that can be used for failover if the primary synchronization server fails.

159. Answer: B

Explanation: If there is sensitive data in the on-premises Active Directory that should not be synchronized to Entra ID, you can use the Azure App and Attribute filtering option in the Entra ID Connect Wizard to exclude the attribute from the synchronization process.

Answers

160. Answer: B

Explanation: After reviewing and confirming the configuration in staging mode, you proceed by disabling the staging mode using the Entra ID Connect Wizard and then enabling the synchronization scheduler. This will start the export of data to Entra ID.

161. Answer: B

Explanation: Password synchronization with Entra ID Connect is designed to replicate password changes from on-premises Active Directory to Office 365 within a short time frame, typically every 1 to 2 minutes. This ensures that any password changes made by users are quickly updated in Office 365, allowing for seamless access to services.

162. Answer: C

Explanation: Passwords synchronized to Office 365 are not transmitted. Instead, the hash of the user's password is encrypted a second time with an MD5 key and a salt to create a salted hash. This salted hash is then transmitted by an encrypted HTTPS session, ensuring the password's security during synchronization.

163. Answer: B

Explanation: In express mode, the service account created during the Entra ID Connect installation is automatically delegated the Replicating Directory Changes and Replicating Directory Changes All permissions. These permissions are necessary for the account to synchronize changes from the on-premises Active Directory to Microsoft Entra ID.

164. Answer: D

Answers

Explanation: Pass-through authentication allows the on-premises Active Directory infrastructure to process authentication requests. Unlike password synchronization, it does not involve transmitting passwords to the cloud, as authentication takes place on-premises.

165. Answer: C

Explanation: The processing agent used for pass-through authentication must be installed on a server that is joined to the domain where the users reside, and the server must be running Windows Server 2012R2 or later to support the feature.

166. Answer: B

Explanation: When using password synchronization, even if a password expires in the on-premises Active Directory, it remains valid in Office 365 because the cloud account password is set to Never Expire. This means users can still log on to the tenant using their current password.

167. Answer: B

Explanation: In a multi-forest configuration to support pass-through authentication, a two-way trust between the forests is required. Pass-through authentication allows users to sign in to Microsoft Entra ID (Entra ID) using their on-premises credentials, and for this to work in a multi-forest environment, there must be a two-way trust relationship established between the forests. This trust relationship enables authentication requests to flow between the forests, allowing users in one forest to authenticate against resources in another forest.

168. Answer: C

Answers

Explanation: For pass-through authentication, the UserPrincipalName (UPN) used for synchronization to Office 365 must be the value from the on-premises Active Directory UserPrincipalName attribute and must be a routable UPN suffix. An alternate Login ID is not supported with pass-through authentication.

169. Answer: C

Explanation: When selecting Federation with AD FS during Entra ID Connect setup, additional installations of the AD FS Federation server role and the Web Application Proxy server role are necessary. These roles are not installed on the Entra ID Connect server but on at least two additional servers prepared for these roles.

170. Answer: B

Explanation: Pass-through authentication is an alternative to password synchronization for companies that prohibit the transmission of passwords, even in an encrypted format, over the public Internet. With pass-through authentication, the on-premises Active Directory processes the authentication requests directly without the need to transmit passwords to the cloud.

171. Answer: C

Explanation: The Entra ID Connect installation wizard necessitates that the forest user name credentials be provided in the DOMAIN\UserName format. This requirement exists because these credentials are stored in the properties of the on-premises Active Directory connector for the synchronization process. Using the UPN format would result in an error, leading to the termination of the installation wizard.

Answers

172. Answer: B

Explanation: Inputting credentials in the UPN format (e.g., dan.park@cohovineyard.corp) during the setup will trigger an error. As a result, the installation wizard will exit, requiring you to restart the entire installation process from the beginning.

173. Answer: B

Explanation: At a minimum, the service account used for directory synchronization needs to be a member of the Domain Users group in Active Directory. Additionally, the account must also have LDAP read permissions to the forests it is intended to synchronize with.

174. Answer: B

Explanation: The additional permissions and requirements for features like Group Writeback and others can be found on the Microsoft official website, You should refer to the documentation there for the most current and detailed information.

175. Answer: C

Explanation: The synchronization rules created by the Entra ID Connect wizard are applied based on the order in which you add directories during the installation process. This is particularly important in multi-forest scenarios.

176. Answer: B

Explanation: If you see a warning about unverified domain suffixes during the installation, it serves as a reminder that additional work may be needed to register domains or align UPN values. However, you can safely proceed

Answers

with the installation, as these suffixes can be verified later without affecting the installation or requiring a re-run of the wizard.

177. Answer: C

Explanation: The default attribute for the UserPrincipalName value for logon and authentication with Entra ID is typically the UserPrincipalName from the on-premises Active Directory schema. However, there may be cases where an alternate attribute is required or preferred.

178. Answer: A

Explanation: The Mail attribute is the most common alternate used for the UserPrincipalName value because both the Mail value and UserPrincipalName typically share the name@domain format. This is known as the Alternate Login ID.

179. Answer: B

Explanation: The selection of the UserPrincipalName attribute during the installation is irreversible. If a mistake is made, the only remedy is to uninstall Entra ID Connect and perform the installation again with the correct attribute.

180. Answer: B

Explanation: A gray check box with a check mark indicates that while not all sub-OUs under the selected OU are included in the synchronization scope, any new OUs created beneath it in the future will be included automatically without requiring changes to the Entra ID Connect configuration.

Answers

181. Answer: C

Explanation: Failing to choose the correct user-matching option in a multi-forest setup can result in improper synchronization, requiring a reinstallation of the Entra ID Connect tool, and might also necessitate deleting incorrectly synchronized objects from Entra ID.

182. Answer: D

Explanation: The mailNickname attribute is critical for synchronizing Exchange mailbox objects to Office 365, as it identifies the account as a mail-enabled object.

183. Answer: C

Explanation: The msExchMasterAccountSID attribute contains the security identifier (ObjectSID) of the user account from the account forest that the mailbox in the resource forest is linked to.

184. Answer: B

Explanation: In a standard Exchange resource forest scenario, the user account in the account forest is enabled and used for logon, while the mailbox account in the resource forest is disabled.

185. Answer: B

Explanation: For linked mailboxes, the msExchRecipientTypeDetails attribute in Active Directory should be set to a value of 2.

186. Answer: C

Answers

Explanation: The Mail Attribute user join configuration is most commonly used when directories contain Exchange mailboxes and global address list synchronization is performed between those forests using Microsoft Identity Manager or Forefront Identity Manager (GalSync).

187. Answer: C

Explanation: When joining user objects using sAMAccountName and mailNickname, these values are expected to be unique within their respective forests.

188. Answer: C

Explanation: If you manually select an attribute for user joins that are not in the Entra ID Connect metaverse, such as sAMAccountName or a custom attribute not defined, the installation will fail with an error.

189. Answer: B

Explanation: The SourceAnchor attribute in Entra ID Connect uniquely identifies an object and anchors it to the source object that it represents in the on-premises directories. It is a critical component that cannot be changed once synchronization has begun.

190. Answer: C

Explanation: When selecting an alternate attribute for SourceAnchor, it is crucial to choose one that will never change, as any alteration would break the synchronization of the object.

191. Answer: C

Answers

Explanation: Sway allows users to generate and import their own content or import content from external sources to create and share their stories within a web browsing session.

192. Answer: C

Explanation: Sways can be shared with your organization's users or posted publicly for external users to discover.

193. Answer: C

Explanation: Access to Sway is configured by user licensing, which involves assigning or removing a Sway license for the user.

194. Answer: C

Explanation: Microsoft To-Do is an app that can be used to manage tasks, which can be grouped into categories and synchronized with Exchange tasks.

195. Answer: C

Explanation: Administrators can configure the password policy for managed accounts by selecting Edit in the Password Policy section, where they can set time limits for password expiration and notification or configure them never to expire.

196. Answer: C

Explanation: The self-service password reset feature is an Entra ID Premium feature and requires an additional license.

Answers

197. Answer: C

Explanation: When you create an Office 365 tenant, Microsoft assigns a data location based on the country or region specified during the setup process. This data location determines where your data is primarily stored and processed. Once set, changing the data location isn't straightforward and may not be possible without significant migration efforts. Therefore, it's crucial to carefully consider the data location when initially creating your tenant to ensure compliance with regulatory requirements and data sovereignty concerns.

198. Answer: C

Explanation: You can apply branding and theme customization to Office 365 to match your organization's branding.

199. Answer: C

Explanation: The Partner Relationships page shows Microsoft partners that you have configured as Partner of Record or Subscription Advisor for your Office 365 subscriptions, which you can add under Billing | Subscriptions.

200. Answer: B

Explanation: To add a new custom tile to the App Launcher for each user, you need to click the +Add A Custom Tile button, specify the required information, and save the changes.

201. Answer: B

Answers

Explanation: A "Plan for Change" notification means that a change is forthcoming in how a feature is deployed or managed. It may imply that a service feature will be deprecated and replaced with a new one. Administrators are notified about the change and provided with appropriate planning tools, a transition or retirement date, and an upgrade path.

202. Answer: C

Explanation: The Exchange Admin Center can be accessed from the Service admin centers in the Office 365 Admin Center. It is one of the individual cloud services admin centers made available for tenant management.

203. Answer: C

Explanation: The Compliance Management section in the Exchange Admin Center is used to create and manage retention policies and tags, manage data loss prevention policies and templates, run auditing reports, place holds on data, and configure journaling.

204. Answer: A

Explanation: Mail Flow settings in the Exchange Admin Center allow administrators to configure accepted domains (domains owned by the organization), transport rules, and connectors to on-premises or other organizations' mail systems. Administrators can also trace messages through these settings.

205. Answer: C

Explanation: The User Profiles page within the SharePoint Admin Center is where you manage settings for user profiles (MySites) as well as organization properties and attributes that SharePoint can work with.

Answers

206. Answer: B

Explanation: Command Logging enables administrators to see the exact Windows PowerShell commands that the admin center runs behind the scenes. This is particularly useful when performing actions in the Exchange Admin Center and wanting to learn the PowerShell equivalent.

207. Answer: A

Explanation: The Hybrid section in the Exchange Admin Center contains a link to start the Office 365 Hybrid Configuration Wizard, which is used to integrate on-premises Exchange with Exchange Online. It also provides a link to download the Exchange Online PowerShell module.

208. Answer: B

Explanation: The "Users" menu in the Skype for Business Admin Center allows administrators to manage individual user settings, including whether a user can use audio or video features within Skype for Business.

209. Answer: B

Explanation: The Term Store settings page in SharePoint Online is where you configure term sets that can be used across your SharePoint tenant.

210. Answer: B

Explanation: The Service Health page in the Office 365 Admin Center provides an overview of the current service status, incidents currently being managed by Microsoft that affect your tenant, and advisories that might be affecting your tenant.

Answers

211. Answer: B

Explanation: The EmployeeID number or other unique company identifiers are good candidates for SourceAnchor, provided the company has a mature Identity Management system to prevent duplication and prohibit reuse. Social Security Numbers, although unique, are PII and have strict legal requirements associated with their use.

212. Answer: C

Explanation: Organizations should work with their legal and corporate security teams before using PII data in synchronization with Office 365 due to the specific laws and requirements associated with PII.

213. Answer: B

Explanation: Most organizations select an alternate SourceAnchor because they are involved in frequent mergers, acquisitions, or divestitures and expect to move objects across forests regularly.

214. Answer: C

Explanation: By selecting one group from each forest during the Entra ID Connect installation, you can filter users, groups, contacts, or devices for synchronization to Entra ID, ensuring that only objects in the selected group are synchronized.

215. Answer: A

Explanation: When filtering objects in Active Directory for directory synchronization, the group used for filtering must reside in a top-level OU

Answers

(Organizational Unit) within the scope of the solution. This ensures that the group and its members are included in the synchronization process. Placing the group in a top-level OU helps ensure that it is easily accessible and that all relevant objects are included for synchronization.

216. Answer: B

Explanation: The Exchange Hybrid Deployment feature enables the Entra ID Connect tool to write back a select number of attributes from Exchange Online into on-premises Active Directory.

217. Answer: B

Explanation: Some features on the Optional Features page of Entra ID Connect may require additional subscriptions, such as Entra ID Premium licensing, to be used.

218. Answer: C

Explanation: The Entra ID App and Attribute Filtering feature allows you to select specific Office 365 workloads for synchronization or to exclude certain attributes from synchronization to Entra ID.

219. Answer: B

Explanation: Clearing an application checkbox in Entra ID Apps filtering removes all outbound rules from the configuration related to that application, thereby preventing attributes related to it from being synchronized to Entra ID.

220. Answer: B

Answers

Explanation: Password Writeback is a feature that enables users to change their passwords in Microsoft Entra ID, and the change is automatically reflected in on-premises Active Directory.

221. Answer: D

Explanation: Password admins have the right to reset passwords, manage service requests, and monitor Office 365 service health.

222. Answer: C

Explanation: Sign-In blocked users usually cannot sign in to Office 365 when Directory Synchronization is enabled. This often happens because their accounts are disabled on-premises.

223. Answer: B

Explanation: The "Add Custom View" option in the Office 365 Admin Center allows you to create a custom view for filtering users based on various criteria.

224. Answer: C

Explanation: Global administrators or Exchange administrators can create shared contacts in the Office 365 Admin Center.

225. Answer: C

Explanation: The Guest Users page in Office 365 typically displays external users who have been added as members of Office 365 groups within the organization's environment. This page provides administrators with visibility into the external users who have been granted access to collaborate

Answers

on documents, participate in teams, or engage in other activities within Office 365 groups. It is a useful feature for managing external collaboration and ensuring proper access controls are in place.

226. Answer: C

Explanation: In Microsoft 365, when a user account is deleted, it can typically be restored within a specified period, usually up to 30 days after deletion. During this retention period, administrators can recover deleted user accounts, along with their associated data, such as emails, files, and settings. This feature provides a safety net in case user accounts are accidentally deleted or if there's a need to restore access to the deleted user's data. After the retention period expires, however, the deleted user account and its data may be permanently removed from the service.

227. Answer: B

Explanation: Room and equipment mailboxes are special types of shared mailboxes that are configured as a specific recipient type in Exchange Online with unique calendar-processing and delegate information.

228. Answer: D

Explanation: The Sites page in Office 365 allows you to perform basic site operations for SharePoint Online, like creating a site collection and administering external sharing.

229. Answer: B

Explanation: Billing admins can make purchases, manage subscriptions, open tickets, and monitor service health in Office 365.

Answers

230. Answer: B

Explanation: Office 365 groups, also known as modern or unified groups, can only be created and managed within Office 365.

231. Answer: C

Explanation: You can add a partner of record on the Subscriptions page in the Office 365 admin center. This is done by selecting the More Actions drop-down list next to the subscription you want to modify and then selecting Add Partner Of Record.

232. Answer: A

Explanation: The first step to sign in to Office 365 with an account authorized to make service changes is to select the App Launcher icon and then click Admin.

233. Answer: D

Explanation: The Subscriptions page lists the purchased subscriptions or SKUs along with details such as the number of license units purchased and assigned, descriptions, and pricing.

234. Answer: B

Explanation: Calendar sharing permissions for the Exchange Online organization can be managed by accessing the Calendar service configuration item within the admin center

235. Answer: B

Answers

Explanation: For Cortana to search Office 365 content on Windows 10 devices, Cortana services must be enabled on the Cortana service setting. Cortana must be configured to allow access to your Office 365 data.

236. Answer: B

Explanation: The Licenses page under Billing in the Office 365 admin center provides a high-level snapshot of the licenses available in your Office 365 tenant.

237. Answer: C

Explanation: To purchase additional services for your Office 365 tenant, you need to navigate to the Purchase Services page, where you can select services and choose Buy Now.

238. Answer: C

Explanation: Billing notifications are sent to administrators listed as global administrators and billing administrators, and the list of these users is dynamically built from these roles.

239. Answer: C

Explanation: To upload an add-in from the Office Store to your Office 365 tenant, you would go to the Services & Add-Ins page and follow the steps to upload and configure the add-in.

240. Answer: C

Answers

Explanation: Azure MultiFactor Authentication controls how users can access your Office 365 tenant, and it can be enabled per-user or by selecting various filters based on administrative roles.

241. Answer: D

Explanation: When Docs.com is not enabled for an organization, any attempt by a user to sign in to Docs.com using their Office 365 ID results in an error message indicating that the service has been disabled for their organization

242. Answer: C

Explanation: As of August 1, 2017, users were no longer able to upload content to Docs.com. This was part of the process leading up to the service being completely turned off later that year.

243. Answer: A

Explanation: GigJam supports integration with a variety of data types, including calendars, contacts, email, opportunities and accounts.

244. Answer: A

Explanation: Integrated Apps are enabled by default in Office 365, allowing users to grant third-party apps access to their Office 365 information, such as calendars or files in OneDrive.

245. Answer: B

Answers

Explanation: Azure Information Protection allows users to apply rights to email messages and documents to control their distribution, effectively enabling them to sign, encrypt, and manage content securely.

246. Answer: B

Explanation: To use Microsoft Teams, individuals must have a separate user license, which is not included by default with all Office 365 plans.

247. Answer: A

Explanation: The Office 365 Groups settings page specifically allows the management of external access to groups, while other configuration options are discussed elsewhere.

248. Answer: A

Explanation: By default, Office Online is set up to work with third-party storage service providers, allowing users to collaborate on documents stored in services outside of Microsoft's ecosystem.

249. Answer: C

Explanation: StaffHub is designed primarily for desk-less workers in service industries, offering them a way to access work-related resources without a full-time workstation.

250. Answer: B

Answers

Explanation: Self-provisioning is a feature in StaffHub that enables users to create their accounts through the application's browser or mobile app interface, simplifying the account creation process.

251. **Answer: C**

Explanation: The correct endpoint for managing Exchange Online Protection via PowerShell is https://ps.protection.outlook.com/powershell-liveid. This specific endpoint is used to import the necessary commands for managing Exchange Online Protection in a PowerShell session.

252. **Answer: B**

Explanation: The Retention Management role enables users to manage retention policies within the Office 365 Security & Compliance Center.

253. **Answer: C**

Explanation: The Audit Logs role allows users to turn on and configure auditing for their Office 365 organization, view the organization's audit reports, and export these reports to a file.

254. **Answer: A**

Explanation: The PowerShell endpoint for the Security & Compliance Center is https://ps.compliance.protection.outlook.com/powershell-liveid.

255. **Answer: B**

Answers

Explanation: The Device Management role allows users to view and edit settings and reports for device management features within the Security & Compliance Center.

256. Answer: A

Explanation: To manage advanced alerts, you should enable Advanced Security Management in Office 365, which allows access to additional alerting features and redirects you to the Office 365 Cloud App Security portal.

257. Answer: A

Explanation: The Compliance Search role enables users to perform searches across various Office 365 locations and get an estimate of the search results. Roles like Export and Preview would be needed for further actions on these search results.

258. Answer: C

Explanation: When content is placed 'on hold,' it is preserved in a secure location even if the content owners modify or delete the original content. The content will be preserved until the hold is removed or the hold duration expires.

259. Answer: A

Explanation: The RMS Decrypt role enables users to decrypt RMS-encrypted email messages when they are exporting search results or preparing search results for analysis in Advanced eDiscovery.

Answers

260. Answer: C

Explanation: The Case Management role enables users to create, edit, delete, and control access to eDiscovery cases within the Security & Compliance Center.

261. Answer: C

Explanation: The Alerts Dashboard with the option to configure analytics is a feature available with an Enterprise E5 subscription.

262. Answer: C

Explanation: To enable Office 365 Analytics, you must go to the Alerts Dashboard and click on 'Enable Office 365 Analytics'.

263. Answer: C

Explanation: If you have licenses that include Advanced Security Management, the View Alerts menu replaces View Security Alerts.

264. Answer: B

Explanation: To start generating alerts on activities, you must enable the recording of activities by clicking 'Start Recording User And Admin Activities'.

265. Answer: B

Explanation: If you have an Enterprise E5 or Advanced Security Management SKU, you can configure Advanced Alerts And Alert Policies by navigating to Alerts | Manage Alerts.

Answers

266. Answer: C

Explanation: To enable auditing for all mailboxes, you must run the cmdlet 'Get-Mailbox -ResultSize Unlimited | Set-Mailbox -AuditEnabled $true' in Exchange Online PowerShell.

267. Answer: B

Explanation: After enabling recording, you must confirm the action by clicking 'Turn On' to enable security auditing.

268. Answer: C

Explanation: A dialog box might appear to update your organization settings, which is the same as running Enable-OrganizationCustomization from Windows PowerShell.

269. Answer: B

Explanation: When creating an alert policy, under 'Send This Alert When', you can expand 'Activities' to select the events that you want to audit.

270. Answer: C

Explanation: When connected to the Security & Compliance Center PowerShell endpoint, you can use New-ActivityAlert and Set-ActivityAlert cmdlets to manage activity alerts.

271. Answer: C

Answers

Explanation: Users assigned to the Security Reader role have read-only access to various security features, such as the Identity Protection Center, Privileged Identity Management, and others, allowing them to view but not modify security configurations.

272. **Answer: C**

Explanation: The View-Only Audit Logs role enables users to view and export their organization's audit reports, which may contain sensitive information; hence, it is suitable for users who need to perform such tasks.

273. **Answer: C**

Explanation: eDiscovery Administrators can perform all case management tasks on any eDiscovery case, even those they are not currently members of, by first adding themselves as a member.

274. **Answer: B**

Explanation: The Service Assurance User role enables members to access and manage Service Assurance documents in the portal, which contain information about service audits and certifications.

275. **Answer: C**

Explanation: To search the Exchange audit logs, a user must assign the necessary permissions in Exchange Online because the search is performed using an Exchange Online cmdlet.

276. **Answer: C**

Answers

Explanation The eDiscovery Manager role group includes two subgroups—eDiscovery Manager and eDiscovery Administrator, each with distinct permissions and capabilities related to eDiscovery cases.

277. Answer: B

Explanation: Reviewers have limited eDiscovery-related permissions, allowing them to see and open only the list of the eDiscovery cases on the eDiscovery page to which they are members and have access.

278. Answer: B

Explanation: Threat Explorer is the feature that enables users to delve into the specifics of individual threats, including their distribution over time and classification by malware families.

279. Answer: A

Explanation: The Supervisory Review Administrator role allows users to create and manage the policies that define which communications are reviewed within an organization, such as for compliance with regulations.

280. Answer: B

Explanation: Incidents within Threat Management are used to track and manage activities related to potential threats, allowing users to review and handle messages or situations flagged as part of an ongoing investigation.

281. Answer: D

Explanation: Safe Links, a security feature in Microsoft Office 365, is not supported in Office Online applications or on Office for Mac, iOS, or

Answers

Android. Safe Links helps protect users from malicious links by checking URLs against a list of known malicious sites and blocking access to them. However, this feature is currently only available in the desktop versions of Microsoft Office applications running on Windows. Users accessing Office documents through Office Online or on mobile devices do not benefit from Safe Links protection.

282. **Answer: B**

Explanation: To enable Safe Links, users need to have an Advanced Threat Protection (ATP) license in their Microsoft Office 365 subscription. This feature provides an additional layer of security by scanning URLs in emails and Office documents for potential threats, such as phishing or malicious links, and blocking access to them. Without an ATP license, Safe Links functionality will not be available to users.

283. **Answer: B**

Explanation: You can review the items in quarantine by navigating to Threat Management | Quarantine in the Security & Compliance Center.

284. **Answer: A**

Explanation: You can filter the quarantined messages based on type, which includes Bulk, Spam, Transport Rule, and Phish.

285. **Answer: B**

Explanation: Access to the Advanced Threats page within Microsoft Office 365 is only available to users with an Advanced Threat Protection (ATP) license. This page provides insights and reports on advanced security threats

Answers

detected within the organization's email and Office 365 environment. Without an ATP license, users won't have access to this page or its features.

286. Answer: B

Explanation: In Microsoft Office 365, you can view and edit scheduled reports by navigating to the "Reports" section and selecting "Manage Schedules." This feature allows administrators to customize and manage the scheduling of various reports, such as usage reports, activity reports, and security reports, providing valuable insights into the organization's Office 365 usage and security posture.

287. Answer: C

Explanation: In the Trust documents section of the Security & Compliance Center, you can find service assurance documents. These documents typically include information related to compliance certifications, audits, and assessments that demonstrate the security, compliance, and reliability of Microsoft's services. They provide transparency to customers regarding Microsoft's adherence to various industry standards and regulations, giving them confidence in using Microsoft's cloud services for their business needs.

288. Answer: C

Explanation: On the Service Assurance | Settings page, you can select which types of assurance documents you want displayed in the portal based on your region and industry.

289. Answer: A

Answers

Explanation: The Compliance Reports page shows several audit and certification reports available for download.

290. **Answer: D**

Explanation: The Audited Controls page shows the standards that Office 365 services have been audited and tested against.

291. **Answer: C**

Explanation: Classifications enable you to categorize and manage the life cycle of information, which includes retaining or deleting content based on policies.

292. **Answer: A**

Explanation: Labels are used to categorize or classify information. Once a label has been created and published, users can apply it to emails or documents to manage content based on retention or deletion policies.

293. **Answer: B**

Explanation: Retention takes precedence over deletion. If content is subject to multiple policies, one that retains content and one that deletes it, the content is retained according to the retention policy.

294. **Answer: C**

Answers

Explanation: If content is subject to multiple policies with retention actions, the content is retained for the longest retention period specified among the policies.

295. Answer: B

Explanation: If content is subject to multiple policies that delete content (with no retention), it will be deleted at the end of the shortest retention period.

296. Answer: C

Explanation: If a user manually applies a label to content, they retain the ability to change or remove the label afterward.

297. Answer: C

Explanation: If content is subject to multiple policies that auto-apply labels, the label for the oldest rule is assigned.

298. Answer: C

Explanation: Labels that are auto-applied based on sensitive information types can only be applied to SharePoint and OneDrive content.

299. Answer: C

Explanation: When creating a label, you can configure both the retention period and the deletion action for the content.

Answers

300. Answer: A

Explanation: Publishing a label for a manual application involves creating a label policy with the selected label(s) as members, making it available for users to use in applications.

301. Answer: B

Explanation:

To apply retention policies to Exchange Online content, you need an Exchange Online Plan 2 license. Exchange Online Plan 2 offers advanced features and capabilities beyond those available in Exchange Online Plan 1, including enhanced compliance features such as data loss prevention (DLP), advanced threat protection (ATP), and the ability to apply retention policies to email messages and other Exchange Online content. While Exchange Online Plan 1 includes basic email functionality, it does not provide access to the advanced compliance features required for retention policies.

302. Answer: C

Explanation: If a user edits or deletes content that's covered in a retention policy in SharePoint, a copy of the content as it existed when the policy was applied is retained in the Preservation Hold library.

303. Answer: B

Explanation: Content in the Recoverable Items folder is retained for 14 days by default. This period can be extended up to 30 days.

304. Answer: C

Answers

Explanation: The contents of an inactive mailbox are still subject to any retention policy that was placed on the mailbox before it was made inactive.

305. Answer: B

Explanation: To preserve content for a minimum of 3 years from when it's created, you must create a policy to retain content for 3 years.

306. Answer: C

Explanation: Preservation Lock is used to help organizations comply with SEC Rule 17a-4, and once enabled for a policy, it cannot be removed or the policy modified, except to extend the retention period.

307. Answer: C

Explanation: If the content in SharePoint is not modified or deleted during the retention period, it's moved to the first-stage Recycle Bin at the end of the retention period.

308. Answer: C

Explanation: A 93-day retention period spans both the first-stage and second-stage Recycle Bins in SharePoint. At the end of 93 days, the document is permanently deleted.

309. Answer: A

Explanation: Retention policies should be used over labels when you need to apply them automatically to all content types in Office 365, including

Answers

Exchange Online mailboxes and public folders, Skype, Office 365 groups, SharePoint, and OneDrive content.

310. **Answer: B**

Explanation: Supervision policies are configured to capture employee communications for examination by internal or external reviewers, which is required in some highly regulated industries for auditing purposes.

311. **Answer: B**

Explanation: The Get-MailboxFolderPermission cmdlet is used to verify the permissions on a folder named for a policy configured under Supervision. When a supervisory review policy is created, a folder is named for the policy, and the reviewer's permissions can be verified with this cmdlet.

312. **Answer: A**

Explanation: Each time a supervision policy is created, a new SupervisoryReview{guid} mailbox is created with a corresponding folder named for the policy inside that mailbox.

313. **Answer: C**

Explanation: When adding a SupervisoryReview mailbox to a user's Outlook profile, the Office 365 button should be selected in the Add Account Wizard.

314. **Answer: C**

Answers

Explanation: After the SupervisoryReview mailbox has been successfully added to reviewers' profiles, you can re-hide it from the global address list if desired.

315. Answer: B

Explanation: To search for user activity in Exchange Online using the Audit Log Search, Exchange mailbox audit logging must be enabled.

316. Answer: C

Explanation: The New-ComplianceSecurityFilter cmdlet is used to restrict the ability of eDiscovery managers to search organizational content by limiting their scope to specific mailboxes or sites.

317. Answer: C

Explanation: The 'New-ComplianceSecurityFilter' command is useful when you need to restrict the search capabilities of an eDiscovery manager to a specific subset of content, such as a particular business unit or department.

318. Answer: B

Explanation: Before users can perform eDiscovery searches, review cases, or export results, they must be added to an eDiscovery-related role group that has the necessary permissions.

319. Answer: C

Answers

Explanation: When an eDiscovery case is closed, any holds that were placed on the content as part of the case are released, which may result in the content being deleted depending on the organization's retention policies.

320. Answer: C

Explanation: The Productivity App Discovery tool is used to gain insights into how users in the organization are utilizing Office 365 and other cloud service applications, which helps provide a more comprehensive view of app usage.

321. Answer: B

Explanation: The initial step in the process of establishing a DLP policy is to determine the type of content that needs to be protected. This is crucial before selecting a policy template or deciding on the locations where the policy will apply.

322. Answer: B

Explanation: To create a DLP policy from a template, you should navigate to the Security & Compliance Center and click on Data Loss Prevention, then select Policy.

323. Answer: B

Explanation: The default setting in a DLP policy is to detect when the content is shared outside the organization. This is to prevent sensitive information from being accidentally disclosed to unauthorized parties.

324. Answer: C

Answers

Explanation: Policy Tips are notifications displayed within the user interface that alert users when they are working with data that matches the criteria set in the DLP policy. They can also be used to report false positives to refine the rules further.

325. Answer: B

Explanation: When a DLP policy is configured in test mode without Policy Tips, the policy does not affect user productivity. Instead, administrators use DLP reports to assess the impact of the policy and tune the rules as needed based on the findings.

326. Answer: C

Explanation: Once you are confident about the configuration of the DLP policy, you can move to full enforcement, where the actions defined in the policy rules are applied to protect sensitive data effectively.

327. Answer: C

Explanation: To modify individual rule settings in a DLP policy template, you can choose advanced settings, which allow for the editing of the template's rules or the addition of new ones.

328. Answer: B

Explanation: To roll out a DLP policy gradually, you can configure the policy in test mode without Policy Tips. This allows you to analyze the impact using DLP reports and make adjustments before fully enforcing the policy.

Answers

329. Answer: B

Explanation: The creation of mobile device management policies requires that the user be logged in with the Global Administrator role, as this provides the necessary permissions to activate and manage MDM services.

330. Answer: B

Explanation: To manage Apple iOS devices with Office 365 Mobile Device Management, you must configure an APNs Certificate, which allows the MDM service to send notifications to the managed iOS devices.

331. Answer: B

Explanation: After activating Office 365 Mobile Device Management, additional security policies and exclusions for the organization can be configured on the Device Security Policies page accessible through Data Loss Prevention.

332. Answer: D

Explanation: Office 365 MDM cannot disable Bluetooth settings directly on Android devices. Instead, it disables all transactions that require Bluetooth.

333. Answer: B

Explanation: Device security policies in mobile device management (MDM) solutions for iOS devices often include the option to block iCloud backup. This feature allows organizations to enforce data protection measures by preventing users from backing up sensitive corporate data to iCloud, thus ensuring data security and compliance with company policies. Additionally, device security policies may offer other options to enhance

Answers

security, such as enforcing passcode requirements, enabling encryption, and restricting access to certain apps or features.

334. Answer: C

Explanation: After PST files are imported, the Retention Hold setting for the mailbox is turned on indefinitely to ensure the mailbox owner or administrator can configure appropriate retention settings.

335. Answer: B

Explanation: The drive shipping method involves purchasing hard drives, copying the PSTs onto them, encrypting them with BitLocker, and then sending them to an Office 365 data center.

336. Answer: A

Explanation: The '+ New Import Job' button appears only after the user's account has been granted the Mailbox Import Export Role.

337. Answer: C

Explanation: The main purpose of the Data Governance section in the Security & Compliance Center is to handle data over its life cycle. This includes implementing policies and controls to manage data retention, protection, classification, and disposal. Data governance encompasses various aspects such as defining data retention policies, applying data loss prevention (DLP) rules, managing sensitive information types, configuring retention labels, and ensuring compliance with regulatory requirements. It provides a comprehensive framework for organizations to effectively manage and protect their data throughout its life cycle, from creation to disposal.

Answers

338. Answer: D

Explanation: EncryptionMethod is not listed as a parameter in the CSV template provided for the PST Import mapping file.

339. Answer: C

Explanation: When importing PST files to user mailboxes in Microsoft Exchange Online, the Workload parameter should indeed specify 'Exchange'. This parameter specifies the workload for which the mailbox import request is intended, ensuring that the import process is appropriately directed to the Exchange service within Office 365. By specifying 'Exchange' as the workload, administrators ensure that the PST files are imported correctly into Exchange Online mailboxes.

340. Answer: C

Explanation: The AzCopy tool is used to copy PST files to an Azure storage blob as part of the network import process.

341. Answer: C

Explanation: After the import job has been completed, the mailboxes are configured with the RetentionHoldEnabled parameter to prevent any retention policy from being processed. When you are certain that your retention policies are correct, you can use the Set-Mailbox cmdlet with the -RetentionHoldEnabled $false parameter to enable the processing of the retention policies on the mailbox.

342. Answer: B

Answers

Explanation: For drive shipping, you must use internal SATA or SAS hard drives. External USB hard drives are not accepted for this purpose.

343. Answer: B

Explanation: If you do not click the Copy The Drive Shipping Key link during the drive shipping import job setup, an error may occur stating that not all of the fields are populated.

344. Answer: A

Explanation: The WAImportExport.exe command is used to prepare the hard drive and copy the PST files to it during the drive shipping import job.

345. Answer: C

Explanation: You should download a copy of the PST import mapping file template or create a CSV file with the specified columns to prepare the PST Import mapping file.

346. Answer: B

Explanation: Enabling an archive mailbox for a user with Exchange Online Plan 2 provides them with unlimited storage space for their archived emails. This feature allows users to store large amounts of email data without worrying about reaching storage limits. It is particularly useful for users who need to retain a significant amount of email data for compliance or business reasons.

347. Answer: B

Answers

Explanation: Retention policies in Office 365 help retain content for a specified period or delete content permanently at the end of a retention period to manage the data life cycle.

348. Answer: B

Explanation: By using the Preservation Lock feature of a retention policy, you can ensure that no one, not even the administrator, can turn off the policy or make it less restrictive, complying with certain regulations like SEC Rule 17aa-4.

349. Answer: B

Explanation: Archive mailboxes can be enabled for all users from the dashboard in the Security & Compliance Center.

350. Answer: C

Explanation: If you select the 'No' button while deciding whether to filter during the drive shipping import process, clicking Next opens the final confirmation page.

351. Answer: C

Explanation: Global Administrators have default access to service health features. To allow another user to view service health, they must be assigned a role that includes service health permissions. While a Service Health Administrator role can access service health features, the Global Administrator role is explicitly mentioned as having this access by default.

352. Answer: B

Answers

Explanation: To assign a service health role to another user, you must first sign in with an account that has Global Administrator privileges.

353. Answer: C

Explanation: To change a user's administrator role, you need to go to the Office 365 portal, select Users, and then edit the roles for the selected user.

354. Answer: D

Explanation: To assign the least-privileged administrative role, you would select the Customized Administrator button and then select the Service Administrator checkbox.

355. Answer: B

Explanation: There are two views of data in the Service Health dashboard: the v1 view, which is the current default, and the v2 view, which contains newer features and data visualizations.

356. Answer: C

Explanation: The 'All Services' tab in the Service Health dashboard presents the current status of all services available to the tenant, regardless of whether they are being used or not.

357. Answer: C

Explanation: Service incidents can be categorized into Planned Maintenance, which are scheduled events communicated ahead of time, and Unplanned Downtime, which are unexpected service interruptions.

Answers

358. Answer: C

Explanation: Advisories refer to service degradations that cause a service to perform at a lower level than normal.

359. Answer: C

Explanation:
The Message Center is the central hub for notifications and summaries of items for Office 365 services.

360. Answer: C

Explanation: 'Plan for Change' messages in the Message Center announce upcoming changes affecting the deployment or management of a service feature, including details about the feature's deprecation and replacement.

361. Answer: C

Explanation: Microsoft Entra ID is the component used by Exchange Online to store attributes and properties for configuration and recipient objects, similar to how Exchange on-premises uses an on-site Active Directory environment.

362. Answer: B

Explanation: In Exchange Online, connectors that control outgoing mail flow are called Outbound (Send) Connectors, and those that control incoming mail are called Inbound (Receive) Connectors.

363. Answer: D

Answers

Explanation: Exchange Online has various types of recipients, including Mailboxes, Contacts, and Distribution Groups, but Nodes are not considered a recipient type.

364. Answer: A

Explanation: Although the cutover migration method technically supports up to 2000 mailboxes, it's more realistic to limit this migration to environments with 150 mailboxes or fewer.

365. Answer: B

Explanation: Staged migrations, suitable for environments with more than 150 mailboxes running Exchange 2003 or Exchange 2007, require the use of Microsoft Entra ID Connect.

366. Answer: B

Explanation: Autodiscover is the process that Microsoft Outlook uses to determine the location of a user's mailbox and is essential for configuring mailboxes correctly in Office 365.

367. Answer: B

Explanation: The first method Outlook uses to locate a user's mailbox is querying the Service Connection Point (SCP) in Active Directory.

368. Answer: C

Explanation: Express migration is suitable for specific scenarios where the on-premises environment is running Exchange 2010, Exchange 2013, or Exchange 2016 and can also be referred to as minimal hybrid migrations.

Answers

369. Answer: D

Explanation: A hybrid migration can be used for Exchange 2010, 2013, or 2016 environments (option B) as well as for environments where Exchange 2007 coexists with an Exchange 2010 or 2013 server (option C). This approach allows for a gradual migration of mailboxes from on-premises Exchange servers to Exchange Online in Office 365 while maintaining some level of coexistence between the two environments.

370. Answer: B

Explanation: In hybrid configurations, Autodiscover DNS records should point to the on-premises mail system initially. This is because on-premises Exchange can redirect requests to Office 365, but Office 365 cannot redirect requests to on-premises Exchange. Once all mailboxes are migrated, the DNS records can be updated to point to Office 365.

371. Answer: C

Explanation: The script available at the Technet link is used to identify conflicting objects by finding all instances of the conflicting address across all object types, which is particularly useful when errors such as duplicate proxy addresses occur during synchronization with Entra ID Connect.

372. Answer: D

Explanation: SSL offloading is used for terminating SSL connections using one or more network devices. It is often configured to manage certificates across multiple servers, particularly in large organizations with server farms.

373. Answer: B

Answers

Explanation: SSL offloading is not supported for Mailbox Replication Service (MRS) traffic because MRS is used for mailbox migrations to and from Office 365 and requires end-to-end SSL encryption of the traffic.

374. Answer: C

Explanation: It is critical to update servers with both Windows and Exchange updates because these updates can bring performance, security, or feature enhancements that are necessary for the migration or coexistence environment to function optimally.

375. Answer: A

Explanation: When on-premises mailboxes are synchronized to Office 365, they are represented by mail-enabled users in Exchange Online. These mail-enabled users have attributes that differentiate them from local mailbox users.

376. Answer: A

Explanation: The relationship between the on-premises objectGuid and the cloud ImmutableID is expressed as a base64 string conversion of the objectGuid to a byte array using the [system.convert]::ToBase64String method.

377. Answer: B

Explanation: The Get-ExchangeCertificate cmdlet is used to view the details of Exchange certificates, including those used for hybrid configuration. It provides information such as the certificate's subject, issuer, validity period, services enabled, and thumbprint..

Answers

378. Answer: C

Explanation: If a mailbox has proxy addresses for domains that are not confirmed in the Office 365 tenant, those addresses must be removed prior to migration, as the migration would fail otherwise.

379. Answer: C

Explanation: To enable successful Autodiscover and cross-premises mail routing during migration, mailboxes need to have a proxy address that matches the tenant's mail routing domain, usually formatted as .mail.onmicrosoft.com.

380. Answer: C

Explanation: The Hybrid Configuration Wizard, as part of the setup process, adds the tenant mail routing domain to all the email address templates that contain domains selected during the hybrid configuration. This is important for mail routing between on-premises and Office 365 mailboxes.

381. Answer: B

Explanation: Microsoft Entra ID plays the foundational role for online services in Office 365, similar to how Active Directory serves for on-premises services.

382. Answer: D

Explanation: To manage Skype for Business Online with PowerShell, you need to download and install the Skype for Business Online Connector module.

Answers

383. Answer: B

Explanation: The Get-MsolUser cmdlet is used to retrieve objects, specifically user objects, within the Microsoft Entra ID.

384. Answer: C

Explanation: Both AzureADPreview and MSOnline modules allow for the management of Microsoft Entra ID objects through PowerShell

385. Answer: B

Explanation: When assigning a license to a user, a location (specified by the -UsageLocation parameter) is required, as it indicates the country where the services are consumed.

386. Answer: C

Explanation: The New-MsolUser cmdlet is used to create a new security principal, or user, in Microsoft Entra ID.

387. Answer: B

Explanation: In Exchange Online, the email properties of a mail-enabled user can be managed through the Exchange Online PowerShell module. This module provides administrators with the ability to perform various tasks related to user mailboxes, distribution groups, and other Exchange Online objects using PowerShell cmdlets. With the Exchange Online PowerShell module, administrators can configure email properties, manage mailbox permissions, set mailbox policies, and perform other administrative tasks efficiently from the command line interface.

Answers

388. Answer: D

Explanation: The Remove-MsolUser cmdlet is indeed used to remove a user object from Microsoft Entra ID (Entra ID). This cmdlet is part of the Microsoft Microsoft Entra ID Module for Windows PowerShell, and it allows administrators to delete user accounts from Entra ID, along with associated attributes and licenses. It's a crucial tool for managing user identities and access in Entra ID environments.

389. Answer: A

Explanation: To use the older version of cmdlets (Microsoft Entra ID 1.0 or MSOnline), it is necessary to have .NET Framework 4.5 or later installed.

390. Answer: C

Explanation: The Connect-MsolService cmdlet is used to establish a connection to the Microsoft Entra ID service within PowerShell.

391. Answer: C

Explanation: Remove-MsolUser cmdlet is used to remove a user from Microsoft Entra ID, and when used with the -RemoveFromRecycleBin parameter, it will also remove the user from the recycle bin.

392. Answer: C

Explanation: To create a contact in the Office 365 Admin Center, you navigate to Users, then Contacts, and use the "Add A Contact" option.

393. Answer: C

Answers

Explanation: The Get-MsolRole cmdlet is used to list all roles available in Microsoft Entra ID (Entra ID). This cmdlet is part of the Microsoft Microsoft Entra ID Module for Windows PowerShell, and it allows administrators to view the roles that are predefined or custom-created within their Entra ID tenant. By using this cmdlet, administrators can retrieve information about roles, including their display names, descriptions, and assigned permissions, which helps in managing access control and permissions within Entra ID.

394. Answer D

Explanation: Resource mailboxes are not a type of group in Entra ID and Office 365; they are a type of recipient in Exchange Online.

395. Answer: C

Explanation: The Add-MsolRoleMember cmdlet is used precisely for that purpose: to add a user to a specific role in Microsoft Entra ID (Entra ID). This cmdlet is part of the Microsoft Microsoft Entra ID Module for Windows PowerShell. It allows administrators to grant permissions and assign roles to users within their Entra ID tenant. By using this cmdlet, administrators can specify the role and the user they want to add to that role, enabling them to manage access control effectively.

396. Answer: C

Explanation: A mail-enabled user is a contact with the features of an Active Directory (or Microsoft Entra ID) security principal.

397. Answer: B

Explanation: The New-MsolGroup cmdlet is used to create a new security group in Entra ID through PowerShell.

Answers

398. Answer: B

Explanation: Setting the RequireSenderAuthenticationEnabled parameter to $false allows the group to receive messages from Internet users.

399. Answer: C

Explanation: An equipment mailbox is a type of resource mailbox used for anything that a user can check out or reserve, such as laptops or projectors.

400. Answer: B

Explanation: Unified groups (also known as Office 365 groups or modern groups) appear as distribution lists when using the Get-MsolGroup cmdlet.

401. Answer: B

Explanation: For customers using Exchange Server 2003 and Exchange Server 2007 without deploying a newer version of Exchange, a Staged Migration is available and recommended, especially if the user count exceeds 2000. This option allows for a more controlled migration process.

402. Answer: B

Explanation: To select the migration type, you navigate to the Exchange Admin Center and choose Recipients | Migration.

403. Answer: C

Explanation: The Full Hybrid Migration is recommended for Exchange 2010, Exchange 2013, and Exchange 2016, as it offers a better user and administrator experience and is designed to work with these newer versions of Exchange.

Answers

404. Answer: C

Explanation: "Available, not recommended" indicates that while the migration option would technically work, it is likely to result in a poor user experience and is, therefore, not the suggested path to take.

405. Answer: B

Explanation: To connect to Exchange Online with Windows PowerShell using multifactor authentication, the Microsoft Exchange Online PowerShell Module that supports multifactor authentication should be installed.

406. Answer: B

Explanation: When configured through the Office 365 Admin portal or the Exchange Admin Center, the normal default setting for MaxConcurrentMigrations is 20. This setting determines the maximum number of simultaneous mailbox migrations.

407. Answer: A

Explanation: The MaxConcurrentIncrementalSyncs parameter specifies the maximum number of incremental syncs allowed at a specified time and must be less than or equal to the MaxConcurrentMigrations parameter.

408. Answer: C

Answers

Explanation: Per tenant, there is a limit of 300 connections for each type of migration: Remote, Outlook Anywhere, and IMAP, which totals 300 MaxConcurrentMigrations connections available.

409. Answer: C

Explanation: The cutover migration process is designed for customers up to 2000 users. If the number of users exceeds this limit, cutover migration is not recommended.

410. Answer: C

Explanation: If the customer has deployed Microsoft Entra ID Connect (Entra ID Connect) and synchronized the directory at least once, cutover migration will be blocked as a migration option in the Exchange Admin Center.

411. Answer: C

Explanation: The migration encountered permissions issues during the cutover process as the administrator did not have the proper permission to access the source mailboxes.

412. Answer: B

Explanation: 15 objects were finalized in the migration process.

413. Answer: B

Explanation: The first post-migration step is to change the MX Record in the customer's public DNS to refer to Exchange Online as the new email endpoint.

Answers

414. Answer: D

Explanation: The internal Service Connection Point (SCP) in Exchange should be removed after the migration, which is required for Exchange Server 2007 and later.

415. Answer: A

Explanation: The staged migration process is designed for customers who are using Exchange Server 2003 and Exchange Server 2007 only.

416. Answer: C

Explanation: The minimum required Office 365 license for the migrated users is an Exchange Online license.

417. Answer: A

Explanation: Unified Messaging on source mailboxes must be disabled before performing a staged migration.

418. Answer: C

Explanation: The migration.csv file is used to specify which user mailboxes will be migrated in a staged Exchange migration.

419. Answer: C

Explanation: If the domain of the user is federated and you set a password in the migration.csv file, an error will occur stating that the password cannot

Answers

be set or the ResetPasswordOnNextLogon property for a federated account.

420. Answer: B

Explanation: The Cutover Migration option is dimmed and unavailable when Entra ID Connect and Directory Synchronization have been enabled because users have been synchronized, which prevents performing a cutover migration.

421. Answer: C

Explanation: Networks are the primary structural and administrative units within a Yammer organization. They consist of collections of groups and users and serve as the space for collaboration.

422. Answer: A

Explanation: The internal network, or home network, is exclusive to users who have a verified corporate address associated with the organization's subscription.

423. Answer: D

Explanation: Yammer has three main admin roles: group admins, network admins, and verified admins. While Office 365 global admins with a matching UPN can inherit the Yammer Verified Admin role, "Global admin" is not a separate admin role within Yammer itself.

424. Answer: C

Explanation: Verified admins can configure network settings, features, and applications, among other rights.

Answers

425. Answer: D

Explanation: Group admins cannot configure network settings as this is a right reserved for network and verified admins.

426. Answer: C

Explanation: https://yammer.com/admin/success takes you directly to the Yammer configuration page.

427. Answer: C

Explanation: The Admins screen is the place where you can assign additional network or verified administrators.

428. Answer: C

Explanation: Users are invited to join the Yammer network through the Invite Users screen.

429. Answer: B

Explanation: The Network Migration screen is used for adding stand-alone Yammer networks or merging networks from another organization into the Office 365 tenant

430. Answer: C

Explanation: Verified admins have the right to read messages in any private group, which is not a privilege accorded to group or network admins.

Answers

431. Answer: C

Explanation: Files and images can be attached to any message or reply, with a limit of 5 GB on each file.

432. Answer: C

Explanation: In Yammer, you can use GIF, JPEG, or PNG images for the network logo. These image formats are commonly supported for logos and other graphical elements across various platforms and applications, including social networking platforms like Yammer.

433. Answer: B

Explanation: A user can be granted Network Admin privileges by typing their name under Appoint Additional Admins in the Yammer Admin Center and clicking Submit.

434. Answer: C

Explanation: Clearing the Org Chart check box disables the building and display of the Org chart in the Yammer user interface.

435. Answer: B

Explanation: The recommended size for the masthead image in Yammer is typically 56 x 1200 pixels. This dimension ensures that the masthead image fits properly and displays correctly at the top of the Yammer network, providing a visually appealing header for the platform.

436. Answer: A

Answers

Explanation: This setting forces users to accept the usage policy upon sign-up and after changes are made.

437. Answer: B

Explanation: Network admins can delete any file in any public group, and group admins can delete files in groups they manage.

438. Answer: B

Explanation: To restrict the creation of external networks to only admins, select the Only Admins button and click Save.

439. Answer: C

Explanation: The recommended size for the email logo in Yammer is typically 50 x 160 pixels. This dimension ensures that the email logo appears crisp and clear when included in email notifications or communications sent through the Yammer platform.

440. Answer: C

Explanation: The first step is to select the gear icon in the Yammer navigation pane and then select your external network.

441. Answer: B

Explanation: The parent network must be enterprise-activated, as mentioned in the context. Stand-alone networks can serve as subsidiary networks, but the parent network requires enterprise activation.

Answers

442. Answer: D

Explanation: During the migration process, only the users from the subsidiary network are migrated, and the groups and content are not. To preserve the content, it must be exported and archived.

443. Answer: C

Explanation: The context explicitly states that Yammer networks that are part of Office 365 tenants cannot be migrated or consolidated.

444. Answer: B

Explanation: The content from the subsidiary's external networks remains available after the migration, while the content from the subsidiary's internal network will not be.

445. Answer: B

Explanation: Only Office 365 global admins have the necessary permissions to perform a Yammer network migration.

446. Answer: C

Explanation: If a user exists in both networks, the account in the parent network will be promoted from a guest to a regular account, and the account in the subsidiary network will be deleted.

447. Answer: C

Answers

Explanation: Data exports are for backup purposes, and there is no functionality to import it back into a Yammer network through the user interface or the Yammer API.

448. Answer: B

Explanation: Before starting a network migration, it is verified that the subsidiary email domain is part of your tenant, and if it's not, you must add it.

449. Answer: C

Explanation: Users and business owners should be notified that the Yammer subsidiary network will no longer be available after the migration is complete, and it is recommended that users back up any important data they wish to keep.

450. Answer: C

Explanation: Network migrations cannot be reversed, and there is no undo button, so planning accordingly is important.

451. Answer: B

Explanation: To access OneDrive for Business Online, one must have a license that includes SharePoint Online or OneDrive for Business, as it is a service typically provided through an organization's subscription to Office 365.

452. Answer: B

Answers

Explanation: OneDrive for Business Online can be accessed by opening a web browser and navigating to https://portal.office.com, where you will find the dashboard with a OneDrive tile.

453. Answer: B

Explanation: The first time you click the OneDrive tile, you see the splash page while your OneDrive for Business site is provisioned, normally taking about 30 seconds.

454. Answer: C

Explanation: When the "Welcome to OneDrive" wizard opens, you should click "Not Now" to cancel it if you wish to proceed without using the wizard.

455. Answer: B

Explanation: To identify which OneDrive sync client you're using, hover over the icon in the system tray, which will differ based on the client version (white cloud for personal or new business sync client, blue cloud for previous business sync client).

456. Answer: B

Explanation: To begin setup for the OneDrive sync client, you can initiate it from either your computer or the Office 365 portal.

457. Answer: A

Explanation: The file name of the new OneDrive for Business sync client is OneDrive.exe.

Answers

458. Answer: A

Explanation: The "Sync Your OneDrive Files To This PC" page is used to choose which folders from OneDrive you want to sync to your PC, or you can select all files and folders by checking the "Sync All Files And Folders In OneDrive" option.

459. Answer: C

Explanation: You can share documents and folders by signing in to the Office 365 portal, clicking the OneDrive tile, selecting a file or folder on the Files page, and then clicking either the "Get Link" or "Share" buttons.

460. Answer: C

Explanation: When you use the "Get Link" option, Office 365 creates a link that grants the recipient edit permission by default, allowing them to modify the file or, in the case of a folder, create, upload, and download files unless the permissions are changed.

461. Answer: A

Explanation: To set up a My Site Secondary Admin, you would navigate to the SharePoint Admin Center and select 'User Profiles.' Under 'My Site Settings,' you would then click 'Setup My Sites.

462. Answer: B

Explanation: The PowerShell command 'Get-ADDomain' is used in conjunction with 'Get-ADForest' to retrieve a list of domain GUIDs, which are then used to restrict PC synchronization to specific domains.

Answers

463. Answer: C

Explanation: Within the OneDrive for Business Admin Center, under 'Device Access,' you can restrict SharePoint and OneDrive for Business access by configuring the option 'Control Access Based On Network Location' to limit access to certain IP address ranges.

464. Answer: A

Explanation: To restrict the sharing of OneDrive content with external users, you would use the toggle 'Let Users Share OneDrive Content With External Users' in the Sharing settings of the OneDrive for Business Admin Center.

465. Answer: B

Explanation: To apply My Site Secondary Admin privileges to existing sites, you must use the script and process described in the provided Technet link, as the setup only affects new sites as we advance.

466. Answer: D

Explanation: OneDrive for Business does not restrict files named with a leading underscore. However, it does restrict files larger than 2 GB, files with a path longer than 400 characters, and files named with a leading period.

467. Answer: B

Explanation: To disable OneDrive provisioning for everyone except certain individuals or groups, you would select 'Everyone Except External Users' in

Answers

the user list and clear the 'Create Personal Site' checkbox. Then, you can add specific users or groups and enable the checkbox for them.

468. Answer: C

Explanation: Removing a user's SharePoint license results in the user losing access to their OneDrive for Business site, which could lead to loss of data stored in the OneDrive site.

469. Answer: C

Explanation: To restrict access on devices or platforms that don't support conditional access policies or modern authentication, you can configure the setting 'Control Access From Apps That Can't Enforce Device-Based Restrictions' in the Device Access settings.

470. Answer: C

Explanation: The maximum file size that can be synchronized through the OneDrive sync client is 2 GB. Files larger than this will not sync and will cause synchronization errors.

471. Answer: B

Explanation: To configure the Managed Metadata service, you must first navigate to 'System Settings' in SharePoint Central Administration and then click on 'Manage Services On Server.'

472. Answer: C

Answers

Explanation: If the Managed Metadata service isn't listed under Service Applications, you should click 'New' from the menu and select 'Managed Metadata Services' from the list to create it.

473. Answer: C

Explanation: Under 'Template Selection', you select the 'Enterprise' tab and then choose the 'My Site Host' template when creating a new My Site Host site collection.

474. Answer: B

Explanation: To enable the User Profile service, you need to navigate to 'System Settings', then 'Manage Services On Server', locate 'User Profile Service', and click 'Start'.

475. Answer: B

Explanation: You should not start the User Profile Synchronization Service at this time because doing so will cause the rest of the configuration steps to fail.

476. Answer: C

Explanation: The App Management service is responsible for storing information regarding SharePoint app licenses and permissions.

477. Answer: C

Answers

Explanation: The SharePoint Foundation Subscription Settings service must be configured with SharePoint PowerShell, which is accessed through the SharePoint Management Shell.

478. Answer: A

Explanation: For a SharePoint Server farm to consume resources and content from SharePoint Online or Office 365, server-to-server authentication must be configured.

479. Answer: B

Explanation: After configuring a new connection, you should start Incremental Profile Synchronization by selecting the 'Start Incremental Synchronization' button.

480. Answer: B

Explanation: To use OneDrive for Business in Office 365, users must have the 'Create Personal Site' and 'Follow People and Edit Profile' permissions.

481. Answer: B

Explanation: The default setting for storage management in SharePoint Online is Automatic Storage Operation, which allows the size of the site collection to grow automatically as it nears its limit. This contrasts with Manual Storage Operation, where an administrator must update quotas for site collections as they grow.

482. Answer: C

Answers

Explanation: The New Experience is the default user interface enabled in OneDrive for Business. Users can still switch to the Classic Experience if they prefer, but the New Experience is set as the standard default interface.

483. Answer: C

Explanation: The default setting for the Sync Client for SharePoint is to Start The Old Client. Although it is recommended to use the new client by selecting the Start The New Client button, the default is set to use the older version of the sync client.

484. Answer: B

Explanation: The default setting for the Admin Center Experience in SharePoint Online is Use Advanced. This setting controls the level of configuration options displayed to the administrator, with Use Advanced providing a broader set of options.

485. Answer: A

Explanation: The default setting for the Enterprise Social Collaboration platform in SharePoint Online is to Use SharePoint Newsfeed. While Yammer is also an option, it is not covered in the Office 365 Trust Center, and SharePoint Newsfeed is set as the default.

486. Answer: C

Explanation: The default setting for Site Pages in SharePoint Online is to Allow Users To Create Site Pages using the authoring canvas. This enables users to build and customize their site pages within SharePoint Online.

Answers

487. Answer: B

Explanation: In SharePoint Online, IRM stands for Information Rights Management. This feature is used to encrypt documents and restrict access only to users who have specific permissions, helping to prevent the unauthorized distribution of documents.

488. Answer: B

Explanation: The default setting for Mobile Push Notifications for OneDrive for Business is to Allow Notifications. This enables users to receive push notifications on their mobile devices for OneDrive for Business activities.

489. Answer: B

Explanation: The default behavior for the Comments on Site Pages setting in SharePoint Online is to Enable Comments On Site Pages. This allows users who have access to view a page to leave comments on it.

490. Answer: C

Explanation: By default, the setting that determines site creation in SharePoint Online is set to allow users to create either A Site With An Office 365 Group Or A Classic Site. This provides flexibility for users to choose the type of site they wish to create, even if Office 365 group creation is disabled.

491. Answer: B

Explanation: Yammer activity can be tracked through the Account Activity admin screen, where administrators can perform session administration activities such as logging off individual user sessions.

Answers

492. Answer: B

Explanation: To log off an active user session, click the Logout link next to the user's name on the Account Activity page.

493. Answer: B

Explanation: When a user's email address is blocked, they cannot join the Yammer network. The blocked user can only register after an admin removes their address from the blocked user list.

494. Answer: C

Explanation: Bounced email addresses are those where messages return non-delivery reports. These are listed and can be deactivated by an administrator if necessary.

495. Answer: B

Explanation: For the Bulk Update feature, the CSV-formatted table must include a header with the fields: Action, Email Address, Full Name, Job Title, Password, and New Email.

496. Answer: C

Explanation: To deactivate a user account in the Bulk Update CSV, you need to place the value 'Suspend' in the action column.

497. Answer: C

Answers

Explanation: Admins can customize the profile page by selecting or clearing checkboxes in the Profile Fields dialog box in the Yammer navigation pane.

498. Answer: B

Explanation: The Monitor Keywords feature is used to generate notifications to an administrator whenever content matching certain patterns, such as sensitive information, is posted.

499. Answer: C

Explanation: When a user with a blocked email address attempts to sign up, they will be unable to complete the process, and instead of being able to complete the signup, the Sign Up Free button changes to Retry.

500. Answer: B

Explanation: The Export Users feature allows the export of a CSV file that includes fields such as User ID, Email Address, Name, Job Title, Location, and the date the user joined the Yammer network.

About Our Products

Other products from VERSAtile Reads are:

 Elevate Your Leadership: The 10 Must-Have Skills

 Elevate Your Leadership: 8 Effective Communication Skills

 Elevate Your Leadership: 10 Leadership Styles for Every Situation

 300+ PMP Practice Questions Aligned with PMBOK 7, Agile Methods, and Key Process Groups – 2024

 Exam-Cram Essentials Last-Minute Guide to Ace the PMP Exam - Your Express Guide featuring PMBOK® Guide

 Career Mastery Blueprint - Strategies for Success in Work and Business

 Memory Magic: Unraveling the Secret of Mind Mastery

 The Success Equation Psychological Foundations For Accomplishment

 Fairy Dust Chronicles – The Short and Sweet of Wonder

 B2B Breakthrough – Proven Strategies from Real-World Case Studies

About Our Products

 CISSP Fast Track Master: CISSP Essentials for Exam Success

 CISA Fast Track Master: CISA Essentials for Exam Success

 CISM Fast Track Master: CISM Essentials for Exam Success

 CCSP Fast Track Master: CCSP Essentials for Exam Success

 CLF-C02: AWS Certified Cloud Practitioner: Fast Track to Exam Success

 ITIL 4 Foundation Essentials: Fast Track to Exam Success

 CCNP Security Essentials: Fast Track to Exam Success

 Certified SCRUM Master Exam Cram Essentials

Copyright © 2024 VERSAtile Reads. All rights reserved.
This material is protected by copyright, any infringement will be dealt with legal and punitive action.

www.ingramcontent.com/pod-product-compliance
Lightning Source LLC
Chambersburg PA
CBHW062312220526
45479CB00004B/1143